la gomera
a guide ...

Tim Hart has lived on La Gomera since
1988, writing, fishing, building himself a
house, and enjoying an uneventful life.
Before then he lived in London, was a
musician and song-writer, and for sixteen
years a member of the internationally
successful folk-rock band Steeleye Span.

la gomera
a guide
to the unspoiled canary island

written & photographed
by tim hart

COLLEY BOOKS

First published in Great Britain in 2004 by
Colley Books,
11, Laud's Road, Crick,
Northampton, NN6 7TJ

All photographs taken on - or off the coast of - La Gomera

Designed by Torsten Bartz

Map of La Gomera painted by Thomas Payr

A catalogue record for this book
is available from the British Library.

ISBN: 0-9547989-0-2

Printed in Great Britain by Butler & Tanner,
Caxton Road, Frome, Somerset. BA11 1NF

CONTENTS

CONTENTS

THANKS

Thanks are due firstly to my wife, Conny, whose support, encouragement and tolerance through the thick-and-thins of putting this book together dwarfs all other contributions.

I am also very grateful to Richard Coleman and Hermione Ainley (Colley), who relieved me of the burden of becoming a businessman; to Torsten Bartz, whose artistic talents and technical know-how turned my ingredients into a feast; to Paddy Dennis, who lured me, after thirty years of black-and-white photography, into the digital wonderland of my Fuji FinePix S602; to Chris Harrison, for his unstinting efforts to keep my computing up to date; to Marcia Knoller, who diligently scoured the text, and whose knowledge of the island filled many gaps in mine; to Willie Kirkham, who corrected my proofs and saved me embarrassment; to David Bramwell, botanist and author, whose dedication to explaining and promoting the natural riches of the Canary Islands I could not have done without; and to Mr Alan Wilson and his team at the Whittington.

And, of course, to La Isla de La Gomera.

PREFACE

This book began in haste - at the urgent request of a local vendor of guide-books and postcards, who wanted something in English, yesterday, because his shop was unexpectedly full of Brits and he had nothing to sell them.

That was the best part of two years ago, but La Gomera's not a hasty place, and anyway I'm too fond of this little island to do it the disservice of a rushed job.

La Gomera will never be a resort island, its geography's against it - it's mostly mountain, there's nowhere to put a proper airport, the best beaches are 50 km from the main harbour, and the difficulty of getting here tends to filter out those who need entertaining - which is its great attraction.

It is primarily a place where people live, most of whom grow things and keep animals as they have always done. For many of them, until recently, Europe was a place somewhere beyond Tenerife where the bananas were sent; and while they are becoming used to foreigners with rucksacks and red faces photographing their goats and tumble-down houses, they remain bemused by the sense of urgency that accompanies them.

In writing this book I have made two very different assumptions about you. The first is that you have an interest in getting out and about and exploring the island. The other, not necessarily in conflict with the first, is that you would like to acquire a thorough knowledge of La Gomera without leaving the beach.

La Gomera
July 2004

INTRODUCTION TO LA GOMERA

The Spanish coast is almost a thousand miles away, and Madrid is closer to Glasgow than it is to La Gomera, but politically the Canary Islands are a part of Spain, as they have been for the past five hundred years, and are thereby part of Europe. Geographically, however, they are a part of Africa; the easternmost island being a mere 120 km off the coast of Morocco, and they are regularly dusted with Saharan sand and get the odd plague of locusts. But spiritually the Canary Islands are South American. Much of the populations of Venezuela and Cuba are of Canary Islands descent, driven there by famine and economic necessity, and the trans-Atlantic family ties remain very strong. The Canarian dialect is peppered with South American words, Canary Islands' music has a decidedly Latin feel, and the Carnival in Tenerife is second only to that of Rio de Janeiro in Brazil.

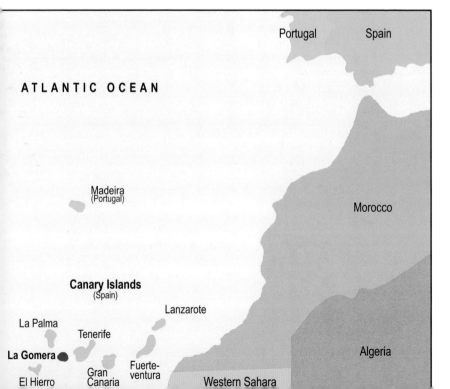

La Gomera is the smallest-but-one of the seven islands in the archipelago, and has long been the secret jewel of the Canaries. It is blessed by being accessible only by sea, and by having no suitable sites for holiday resorts; and it has also been the unspoken policy of those who have discovered it to keep quiet about it - Heaven forbid that the barbaric hordes on Tenerife should invade its peace and tranquillity! Although there is not a great deal on La Gomera to attract the lager-and-chips brigade: or as one off-course English tourist was famously heard to complain; "There's nuffin to do 'ere 'cept the sceeenery!"

Not true of course, but it *is* La Gomera's consistently spectacular scenery, along with its peace and tranquillity and a very old-fashioned pace of life, that inspires visitors to want to protect its fragile magic from the outside world. There are no traffic-lights or dual-carriageways, no roads straight enough to use top gear, no advertising-hoardings, and it's not possible to karaoke the night away. But there are abundant bars, restaurants and accom-

modation to suit every taste and budget, the natives are friendly and hospitable, and a wide variety of beaches provide everything from baby-safe lapping waves to surfable Atlantic rollers.

Introduction

The island itself is actually the top third of a very large mountain whose foothills lie a couple of miles beneath the waves, and it is virtually circular and about 25 km in diameter. Roughly speaking, it consists of a wheel of rocky spokes radiating from a hub higher than Ben Nevis, that separate deep valleys known as *barrancos*. Its centres of population are scattered around the coast at the mouths of these barrancos, and the only way between them by road is to wind your way to the top of the island, go round a bit, and wind your way down again. This means that the distance between any two centres of population is about 50 km and takes about an hour.

La Gomera has remained relatively unspoiled and unaffected by the outside world because throughout most of its history it has been a neglected backwater of the Spanish Empire - it was even forgotten on the map on the euro banknotes, and it suffers the indignity of being the butt of Spanish 'Irish' jokes. Its limited resources meant that the best of its natives were always forced to seek their fortunes far from home, while the fortunes of their island were dictated by world events over which it had no control. Its crops were imposed and controlled by outsiders, and when their markets declined, production on La Gomera was the first to be abandoned.

Until recently, a British tourist was a rare sight on La Gomera, and in this small book, the first guide to La Gomera written in English, I have endeavoured to cover the major points of the many different facets of the island as comprehensively as space allows, and to help you find your way about and get the most out of your visit. I have also tried to convey something of the attitude of mind that underlies the way of life on La Gomera - a place where it's safest to translate 'mañana' as 'not today' - as it has no experience of the pell-mell urgency of Europe and can at times be frustratingly laid-back.

And if you do fall in love with La Gomera, make it a secret affair.

It is the benefits of these centuries of neglect that the visitor enjoys today - the most notable example being that the sugar refineries of the sixteenth century consumed vast amounts of firewood, but because La Gomera came late to growing sugar-cane and retired early it was not required to destroy all of its primeval forests, unlike the other Canary Islands, and what was spared is now the gloriously unspoiled and rigorously protected Parque Nacional de Garajonay that crowns the island.

The LAUREL FOREST is exuberant and made by many evergreen tree species. In the Canary islands grows in the northern slopes of the mountains favoured by the humidity of the trade winds. This forest is a remnant of the vegetation that covered the mediterranean basin in the Tertiary. It become extinct during the Glaciations except in the subtropical environments of the Atlantic islands.

HISTORY

Around 400BC, Pliny the Elder called the archipelago the Fortunate Islands; the Romans gave Gran Canaria its name and called La Gomera Junonia Minor; but it seems most probable that the first settlers of the Canary Islands came from the Berber tribes of Morocco in the first or second century BC.

Quite apart from the geographical logic of this assumption - the Canary Current rises off Morocco and flows southwards between the islands - there is a Berber tribe called Ghomerah, and on La Gomera itself the names of the villages of Agulo and Tazo correspond to the Berber villages of Agulu and Tasa, while Alajeró and Alojera clearly have names of Arabic origin. Although the Berbers are not really Arabs, and can be fair-haired and blue-eyed, which tallies with the descriptions of the natives by the first European visitors.

These first settlers are collectively known as Guanches (which was the Guanche word for 'men'), and once they arrived they appear to have forgotten how to travel by sea, and each island developed its own distinctive culture. They lived in caves, kept pigs and goats, and ate a toasted flour called *gofio*, which is still a Canarian staple and sold in most supermarkets. We are told that the Guanches of La Gomera worshipped a sky-god called Arahan, but theirs was a Stone Age culture which left little in the way of archaeological remains, and was all but wiped out when the Europeans began arriving in the fifteenth century.

La Gomera managed to resist invasion until the late 1440s, when the Spanish nobleman Fernán Peraza, who was already in possession of Lanzarote, Fuerteventura and El Hierro, and whose wars were described as "squalid affairs waged against Neolithic savages", managed to establish a foothold where San Sebastián now stands and built himself a "comfortless keep of stone". This keep, now known as *El Torre del Conde* or the Count's Tower, still stands, and here the Perazas shut themselves up as they sustained a relationship of mutual fear with their vassals, who by the 1480s were staging regular rebellions against their lords and the tributes they demanded.

In 1488, these disturbances culminated in the murder of the young Count of Gomera, Hernán Peraza. The story is that he had been conducting a clandestine affair with a Guanche princess called Yballa, but her suitor Hautacuperche found out and ambushed and killed him at the place now called Degollada (the place of slaughter) de Peraza, 16 km above San Sebastián on the road to Valle Gran Rey.

This sparked off a full-scale rebellion, which was put down by Pedro de Vera, the governor of Gran Canaria, with 400 veteran soldiers. And it was put down with awesome brutality. All Gomero Guanches were deemed equally guilty, including 300 who were living on Gran Canaria; those over fifteen were executed with great cruelty, and the children were sold into slavery.

Part of this barbarity was blamed on the vindictiveness of Beatriz de Bobadilla, Hernán Peraza's beautiful widow, who had been besieged in the Torre del Conde; but such were the excesses that even Ferdinand and Isabella, the rulers of Spain, were appalled. A committee of enquiry was established, and after lengthy deliberations centred on the question of whether Guanches had souls, Pedro de Vera was admonished and the enslaved Gomeros released - in Spain, from where they had to find their own way home. But their native land was now subdued, and by 1500 it was growing sugar-cane for the 'Catholic Kings'.

In 1492, four years after being besieged in her tower, the beautiful Beatriz de Bobadilla played hostess to Christopher Columbus, and was probably the reason he made San Sebastián his last port of call before setting off to discover America. A romance

Columbus

is assumed, as he returned the following year and again five years later; so it is thanks to her charms that La Gomera acquired its place in history.

1492 was also the beginning of the high-point of Spanish fortunes. The marriage of King Ferdinand of Aragon to Queen Isabella of Castile had united the country for the first time, they had driven the Moors out of Granada after almost eight hundred years of occupation, and the discovery of their American colonies and the exploitation of their treasures promised to make Spain rich and powerful. Instead, as the result of a quite incredibly determined display of incompetence, corruption and apathy at all levels of Spanish life, which need not concern us here, the country was bankrupt by 1557 and never really recovered.

As Don Quixote's side-kick Sancho Panza's grandmother used to say: "There are but two sorts of families in the world, the haves and the have-nots," and for the next 500 years the Gomeros were members of the have-nots. Like the rest of the western Canary Islanders, they moved from growing sugar for Spain to producing wine for England, then to scraping cochineal bugs off

History

prickly-pear cacti to dye things red, and most recently to growing bananas; and in the days when tuna were plentiful they caught and canned them. They kept goats and pigs, caught fish, ate *gofio*, grew their own fruit and vegetables, and lived simply and unobtrusively, content to let the world pass them by. Those who did manage to leave the island, the adventurous and the ambitious, the most vital elements of each generation, seldom returned, with the result that the remaining population, depleted in every sense, lacked the drive to do much more than subsist.

Which is why on La Gomera time appears to have stood still.

CLIMATE

For a small island, La Gomera has a lot of climate. The south, roughly from San Sebastián to beyond Santiago, enjoys more than 3,000 hours of sunshine a year, producing an arid landscape with sparse vegetation. The north, around the area of Vallehermoso, Agulo and Hermigua, gets about 2,000 hours of sun, but also spends a lot of time being rained on and is luxuriant. While Valle Gran Rey in the west gets the best of both worlds. For comparison, Northern Europe gets about 1,500 hours of sunshine in a good year.

To further complicate matters, the climate changes vertically as well, and the famous Canary Islands' climate is really only dependable around the coast.

As you would expect with a mountain, it gets cooler, windier and wetter the higher you go, changing in quite distinct bands, until you reach the clouds on which the subtropical rainforest that crowns the island depends.

But generally speaking the weather conditions are ideal, particularly around the coast, where the temperature rarely strays more than 5° from 21°C (70°F). It is usually sunny and warm enough for sunbathing throughout the year, while the Trade Winds bring a steady cooling breeze from the northeast so it seldom becomes unbearably hot.

The occasional patches of bad weather rarely last long enough to spoil an entire holiday; however, the possibility of their occurrence should not be overlooked.

THUNDERSTORMS

These can occur at any time between November and March, and are spectacular events, particularly the thunder echoing in the narrow barrancos. They send the sea crashing over the sea-walls, sweep away the beaches, create waterfalls, rockfalls and roaring stone-filled torrents, block the roads, disrupt the ferries, and knock out the electricity - and deliver a year's supply of irrigation water in a few violent hours, for which the natives readily forgive them the damage they do.

Most years there is at least one, and without them to fill the reservoirs there would be little agriculture on La Gomera.

Weather

LA CALIMA

La Calima is a vast cloud of very fine sand kicked up by storms in the nearby Sahara Desert, sometimes carrying locusts with it, and does nobody any good. It drifts across and envelopes the island in a brown mist from the summit to the sea, so there is no escape; in fact it gets worse the higher you go. The sun is reduced to a vague milky disc, it can become oppressively hot, flu-like symptoms abound, and delicate electronic equipment clogs up.

They usually last between two and five days, often terminate in a shower of rain that leaves a layer of sticky reddish mud over everything, and can occur at any time of the year, but mostly in July and August.

African Locust in a Gomera garden

THE WIND

The wind comes fresh off the Atlantic whichever way it blows, and can at times be considerably fresher than is comfortable - unless it blows off the Sahara, in which case it is called *el Levante* and is hotter than is comfortable as well.

Night Sky

NIGHT SKY

There are major observatories on the peaks of Tenerife and La Palma, sited there because of the clearness of the Canary Islands' sky. But you don't need a telescope to enjoy the stars. Get away from the street lighting on any clear night, find a comfortable place, lie back, and look up.

What looks like a long strip of thin cloud that doesn't move is the Milky Way. The Ecliptic, the line followed by the sun, the moon, the planets, and all the signs of the Zodiac, is high in the sky throughout the year. The very bright planet that appears around sunset or sunrise is Venus; the other really bright one is Jupiter; Sirius, the brightest star in the heavens, is visible throughout the winter; and usually you don't have to wait very long to see a shooting-star.

New Moon & Venus

OLD VOLCANOES

La Gomera is an agglomeration of long-extinct volcanoes, each one now marked by a volcanic plug. These plugs were once the secret hearts of the volcanoes, the last bits of lava of their final eruptions that failed to be expelled and solidified in their gullets, sometime between seven and twelve million years ago. Since then most of the volcanoes themselves have crumbled away, leaving their last gasps standing proud and spectacular.

The most dramatic examples are Los Roques, in the centre of the island above Santiago, a collection of four gigantic menhirs, Agando, Zarcita, Ojila and Carmona, all at around 1,200 m. The Roque Cano (650 m) that towers above Vallehermoso is equally impressive, and the Roque de Sombrero (672 m), visible from the southern road out of San Sebastián, is a smaller but classic example that does indeed look like a hat.

In simple terms, La Gomera consists of a jumble of strata of volcanic outpourings of varying thickness and colour, so convoluted that even seasoned vulcanologists have difficulty disentangling one volcano from another. The lava flows are of the same material and colour as the plugs, usually have a fracture line about a third of the way up that occurred as they cooled, and can create a mass of hexagonal columns as they have at Los Órganos on the north coast.

Most of the rest of the layers consist of solidified ash known as pyroclasts, and are various shades of reddish brown; the finest of which is called *tosca* and is used for building, sculpture, and making ovens. There are also white, yellow and red (usually baked earth) layers, and veins of quartz. The many caves that perforate these pyroclasts were

Roque Cano

caused by pockets of gas.

But the most awesome features are the vertical lava-filled cracks in the cliffs that occurred when earthquakes split the mountain from top to bottom.

Roque Agando

Roque de Sombrero

San Sebastián

SAN SEBASTIÁN DE LA GOMERA

If you were to judge La Gomera from the sight that greets you as you sweep into the harbour of **San Sebastián**, you could be forgiven for thinking it to be a barren and uninteresting island. However, what you are actually doing is more like entering a royal palace via the tradesman's entrance, as you will discover.

The luxury Parador Hotel perches prettily among palm-trees and bougainvillaeas on top

of the cliff on the north side of the bay, and Christ amidst the radio masts atop the hill on the south side makes a thought-provoking grouping. But this is the dry side of the island, mostly covered with spurge, scattered palm trees and agaves, and the town itself was not designed with its visual impact from the sea in mind. On one side lies an industrial estate, on the other, functional housing in pastel shades sprawls up the steep side of the valley, and the town centre is dominated by a particularly ugly tower block.

But San Sebastián is a bustling little town and not without its charms, and as well as being the capital of La Gomera and the only place with a reasonable selection of shops, it contains the only places of historical interest on the island and is worthy of exploration.

The oldest building is **El Torre del Conde** (the Count's tower) to the south of the plaza, built around 1450 to protect the conquerors from the conquered, and still standing despite years of neglect. Until a few years ago it was surrounded by bananas and home to a donkey and some

MAP OF
SAN SEBASTIÁN
INSIDE BACK COVER

San Sebastián

chickens, but it has now been spruced up and a park laid out around it. It was here, in 1492, that Christopher Columbus is reputed to have enjoyed the charms of Beatriz de Bobadilla, the Countess of La Gomera, while provisioning his ships before sailing the ocean blue. Pure speculation of course, the only historical fact is that they knew each other; but she was a notoriously attractive widow stuck in a remote place, and he was a gallant sea captain about to set off into the unknown, so it seems plausible.

He may even have confessed his sins in an early version of **La Iglesia de la Asunción**. This large

San Sebastián

El Torre del Conde

and gloomy church, situated half-way up the right-hand of the two main streets, has been described as one of the main artistic monuments of the island and its façade as Late Gothic. It is certainly of interest, particularly its carved wooden altars. A decaying mural in the far left corner depicts a sea battle that occurred in San Sebastián harbour in 1743, when an attack by the British Admiral Charles Wyndham was repulsed.

By then the residents of San Sebastián had become quite adept at dealing with threats from the sea, but in 1618 Algerian pirates virtually destroyed the church, and the tiny **Ermita de San Sebastián** a little further up the road, recently restored to its original (1450) form, was destroyed at least three times.

There are a number of other buildings of architectural and historical interest along the two main streets of the town, which also contain most of the capital's shops, hotels, pensions, bars and restaurants. The older houses were built around a central court-yard, and it's worth taking a peep through open doorways at the sunny plant-filled interiors as you pass by.

Connections with Columbus (Cristóbal Colón in Spanish) should, however, be taken with a pinch of salt, as pirate raids flattened the town several times after he headed west, and he'd been dead for a century before the Casa Colón was built.

If you allow an hour for your exploration, you should have time to take in a coffee on the adjacent Plaza de la Constitución and Plaza de las Américas as well. This chaotically laid-out open space is the focus of the social life of San Sebastián - it is here that people arrange to meet and where fiestas and concerts are held, the administration of the island runs from the buildings below the clock, and there is a market every Wednesday and Saturday selling local produce.

San Sebastián has two sandy beaches, the 400m Playa de San Sebastián that occupies a large part of the bay, and the recently created Playa de la Cueva just around the cliffs by the harbour.

Plaza de la Constitución

San Sebastián

Apart from the two ends of the main road around the island, two smaller roads lead out of San Sebastián.

If you follow signs for **Cheje-lipes**, at the far end of the town to the sea, you first have an un-promising straight run through an industrial estate, but then the road turns left and right, and thereafter snakes its way up through the pretty villages of the Barranco de la Villa; until it peters out at **La Laja**, below the gigantic menhirs of Los Roques.

The narrow winding road that leads up past the Parador Hotel, continues to the formerly-beau-tiful Playa Avalo. Until recently this was a nature reserve sup-posedly protected by a law passed in 1994. It is now an

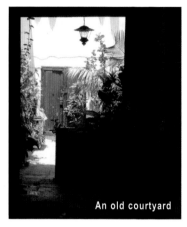

An old courtyard

abandoned building site, and affords such scenes of wanton environmental destruction and ugliness that I only tell you about it so you don't bother to explore in that direction.

La Iglesia de la Asunción

San Sebastián to Garajonay

TOUR AROUND THE ISLAND

The geography of La Gomera makes describing the places of interest in any strict logical sequence impossible. I have therefore chosen to follow the main road around the island in a clockwise direction, followed by diversions to places such as Valle Gran Rey and Playa Santiago which lie at the mouths of long barrancos.

From **San Sebastián** you take the road along the sea-front and round to the right, and then turn left over the bridge,

signed **Valle Gran Rey** 50 km - and as a measure of the bends ahead, Valle Gran Rey is 22 km away as the crow flies.

You spend the next 16 km climbing along the steep sides of dry barrancos ribbed with long-deserted terraces, past the appropriately named Roque de Sombrero and the lion-like Roque de Berrugo, until you reach **Degollada de Peraza**, where there is a large and bleak bar-restaurante with bird's-eye views.

A little way past here the first

Roque de Sombrero

Chejelipes

diversion occurs, to **Playa San-tiago**. [Page 52] The view from the lay-by opposite this junction is well worth a pause: from here you look down on the reservoirs of Chejelipes to your right, and a footpath leads to the houses of La Laja a long way below you.

Continuing along the main road, small trees start to cover the mountainside, and after about 3 km there is a turning to the right to **La Ermita de las Nieves**. This is a small chapel dedicated to the Virgin of the Snows, around which there are many rustic tables and benches, and a large covered array of barbecues and

a kiln-like oven. From here you have a panoramic view of Tenerife.

A couple kilometres further on, after driving through deep man-made ravines carved through solid rock, you reach the awesome monoliths of **Los Roques**: Agando, Zarcita, Ojila and Carmona. [see Old Volcanoes] Here, without a doubt, you should pause and enjoy the views. To your left a footpath descends through pine trees to the village of Benchijigua, and to your right lies the Barranco de la Laja, above which you can often enjoy the sight of cloud cas-

San Sebastián to Garajonay

cading like giant waterfalls over the mountainside. And what stands above you is equally breathtaking - the top of the Roque de Agando is the best part of 200 m above your head, and 1,250 m above the sea.

You should also admire the road itself, constructed with great difficulty and ingenuity about twenty years ago - but remain aware that it is a main road as you nip between view-points or walk backwards to take a photo, too many accidents occur here.

In one of the lay-bys there is a monument commemorating the 20 men, including a newly elected mayor from Tenerife, who died at this spot in 1984. They, however, were watching the fighting of a forest fire in the valley below, when the wind suddenly changed and they were engulfed before they had a chance to flee.

This is probably the windiest place on the island, and also the beginning of the real beauty of La Gomera. You are now in the **Parque Nacional de Garajonay**, you soon begin to enter the forest, and as you do a road leads off to the right to Hermigua. This passes through the magnifi-cent laurel forest known as **El Cedro**, through which there are many wonderful walks.

Continuing along the main road, you climb via a series of tight bends through thickening forest until you come to the **Mirador de Tajaque**, and from this point the road remains relatively level for the next 20 km as it follows a ridge across the centre of the island; and is thus known as the *Carretera Dorsal*. From the Mirador de Tajaque you have on one side a panoramic view of the arid southern slopes of La Gomera, and on the other an equally panoramic view of the verdant north.

3 km further on you come to a junction at a place called **Pajarito**, where a turning to the left to Alajeró and Chipude provides access to the villages on the 1000 m high plateau above Valle Gran Rey. [Page 58]

From Pajarito, the main road curves around **Garajonay**, the highest point and virtually the centre of the island, and you soon come to a parking place on your right. This is El Contadero, so called because here goats were once herded through a narrow gap to be counted. Across

LOS ROQUES

Agando

Zarcita

Ojila

Carmona

San Sebastián to Garajonay

the road is a broad path leading to the top of the mountain - Alto de Garajonay - and from here, on a clear day, you can see the islands of Tenerife, El Hierro, La Palma, and sometimes Gran Canaria, as well as the forested crags and slopes of La Gomera.

Heather-tree blossom

A Guanche legend tells that Gara was a Gomera princess, and Jonay was her lover from Tenerife who paddled across to visit her on inflated goatskins. But her parents disapproved of the match. So they climbed to the top of the island and impaled each other on lances of laurel wood, and their names became one.

From El Contadero, a steep footpath leads down through the heather-trees to the laurel forest of El Cedro, and thence to Hermigua.

From here the road continues to wind through the forest, forest-trails lead off to your left, and after about 3 km a narrow road branches to the right signed Las Rosas and Agulo, which also leads to the **Centro de Visitantes**, or Visitors Centre, at a place called Juego de Bolas. This is the official showcase for the Parque Nacional, and a must for every visitor, but best visited early in the day before the coach parties arrive. It consists of a number of buildings containing exhibits explaining the history, geography, geology, biology, and everything else you could want to know about La Gomera and the Parque Nacional. On display are ancient

The tree on the top of La Gomera

looms, pottery, a wine-press, and reconstructed traditional Gomero houses full of rural artefacts; and the gardens are filled with plants - clearly labelled in Spanish and English - that are either only to be found here or play an important role in traditional Gomero life.

Just after the turning to the Centro de Visitantes you reach La Laguna Grande on your left, where a short road leads you down to the car park.

El Teide from Garajonay

La Laguna Grande

La Laguna Grande means the big lake, and very occasionally, after a particularly heavy downpour, it does indeed fill with a few centimetres of water for a couple of days. But for most of the time it is a broad, grassy recreational area with a couple of rustic children's playgrounds, encircled by barbecue ovens and surrounded by beautiful forest.

Situated in the middle of the island, 1,200 m above the heat of the coast and the focus of many paths, this large and surprisingly level clearing has been a favourite summertime gathering place for Gomeros since time immemorial. On summer weekends these barbecues become the centres of large family fiestas with much eating, drinking, singing and playing of guitars.

For birdwatchers, the trees and bushes surrounding the area provide a cacophony of finches, including the joyous songs of flocks of canaries. In fact this is probably the most reliable place on the island to see them.

If you explore beyond the far side of the grassy area, you will find tastefully constructed woodland paths that lead you through moss-covered and lichen-draped heather-trees (and explanatory notices in Spanish and English); and in the springtime the forest floor is carpeted pink with Canary cranesbill *(Geranium canariense)* and dotted with Madeira sweet violets *(Viola maderensis)*.

There is a bar-restaurante to the right of the car park, which is open during the day and serves generous portions of excellent food. But this is a favourite stop for coach tours, which have to park by the main road, and if you are able to plan your own itinerary it is more enjoyable when the coaches have gone.

It is also more enjoyable if you take a pullover, as even in the summer, clouds can swirl through the trees causing the temperature to suddenly drop from sweltering to nippy.

Canary Cranesbill

Canary

Gomera Cineraria

Epina & Vallehermoso

From La Laguna Grande, you continue along the mostly level and winding road through the Parque Nacional, passing a turning to Las Hayas on your left, followed by signs to **Las Creces** and **Cañada de Jorge**, which are both very pleasant places for a stroll. [see Walks] And after a rare straight stretch of road you come to the turning to **Valle Gran Rey** [Page 64] at a place called Apartacaminos. If you park here and walk into the forest opposite the junction, you will immediately find yourself among gnarled and ancient trees thickly covered with dark green moss and bedecked with lichen.

From here the road starts to descend, and in 3 km you reach the ancient **Chorros de Epina**. The *chorros* are seven wooden pipes protruding from the mountainside from which some of the best spring water on the island pours into a stone trough, and it is worth saving your visit until you have finished at least one large plastic bottle of drinking water and to refill it here. You can drive down a paved road as far as the chapel, and then walk down the steps to the chorros, which is also a barbecue/picnic area.

You are now leaving the forest, views are starting to appear again, and a few bends past Epina there is a turning to your left to Alojera and Taguluche. [Page 76]

From here the road (one of the

Chorros de Epina

La Quilla

oldest on the island, built in the days when obstacles were negotiated rather than bulldozed out of the way) starts to wend its way down into the 'beautiful valley', which is how Vallehermoso translates.

You descend through the villages of La Quilla and Los Bellos, where, like the rest of the valley, the houses are clustered on rocky outcrops safe from the winter torrents. Between them is a turning to Macayo, a small village in a narrow barranco with a picturesque reservoir.

Vallehermoso is a broad valley containing many smaller valleys that focus on the town of the same name, and a hundred years ago this fertile fan of barrancos with their varied agriculture and abundant water (this is the rainy north of the island) made it the richest community on La Gomera. Pears, apricots, potatoes, apples, bananas, plums, grapes and sweet-chestnuts still grow in profusion, and excellent wines are produced; but now the commercial centre has moved to San Sebastián, the harbour has all but vanished, and the remnants of Vallehermoso's former glory look a little tarnished.

If you turn left when you reach Bar Los Órganos, and follow the sign to the optimistically named **Parque Maritíma**, in 3 km you come to where the harbour used to be. This was long ago reclaimed by the sea and only a

Vallehermoso

few structures beyond the reach of the winter waves remain. But undaunted, a large, bright-blue municipal swimming-pool has recently been built behind the shingle beach; and to the left, an ancient fortification has been imaginatively restored to become the arts-centre **Castillo del Mar**, which is spectacularly lit at night, and an interesting place to pause for a snack in the daytime.

Turning right at Bar Los Órganos, following the signs to Agulo, you come into the centre of **Vallehermoso**, which remains in many ways much more of a town than San Sebastián, particularly in the difficulties of finding

Castillo del Mar

your way around its narrow streets. You enter through the more unattractive part of town, and arrive at a small plaza where the two main barrancos, Ingenio and Macayo, meet. Here stands a small town hall with flags flying outside, and a bust of Pedro García Cabrera, a local poet who opposed Franco.

This is the most convenient area to park if you want to explore. The church of San Juan Bautista (John the Baptist) was built in 1902-9 to replace one built in 1635, which burned down due to over-enthusiastic use of votive candles. Also of interest is the children's playground, a brave attempt to blend art and function. The swings and roundabouts stand amid large concrete statues representing 'parent figures', but it is seldom used because the children of Vallehermoso don't like all the concrete and they can't play ball games.

If you continue past the town hall and bear to the right, you will find signs for the **Barranco de Ingenio**. This is a very narrow but very pretty road that leads back up the centre of the valley, through villages that take great pride in their displays of flowers,

The playground

to **La Embalsa de la Encantadora** (the Reservoir of the Enchantress), a large lake fringed with cane and palm trees. Here you can spend a pleasant day fishing for carp and zanders, swimming in fresh but often muddy water, watching ducks and picnicking; there is even a children's play-area. It's also a good place from which to take extended strolls.

If you turn left at the square by the town hall and follow the signs for Agulo, you cross the barranco and leave the town via a short tunnel. Then you drive below **Roque Cano** (650 m), a volcanic plug that the young men of Vallehermoso are supposed to climb to prove their manhood, which dominates every view of the town despite being 1 km away from it.

La Embalsa de la Encantadora

Vallehermoso

You then pass through the Túnel de la Culata, past the scattered houses and terraces of **Tamargaga** - considered to be the purest old Canary village in the archipelago - and round the headland to the scattered houses of **Las Rosas**.

Here, the first road to the right leads to another reservoir stocked with zanders, and then connects to the second road to the right, which winds up to the Centro de Visitantes, and thence to La Laguna Grande and Garajonay.

From Las Rosas, the newly-constructed main road descends dramatically down the steep-sided Barranco de Las Rosas, and after passing through a tunnel you are greeted with the unexpected sight of the clustered houses of Agulo.

Vallehermoso

Roque Cano and La Iglesia de San Juan Bautista

Agulo

Agulo is a very pretty little town set in a fertile cove in the mountainside 200 m above the sea. Its narrow cobbled streets and brightly painted houses are best explored on foot, and you can usually park by the post office on the far side of the town.

The most distinctive building is the multi-domed church of San Marcos, built around 1920 by Pintor y Oceta, the same team who designed the church in Vallehermoso, which contains an early 17th Century Madonna, La Virgin de Merced. On the 24th April, St Mark's day, a fiesta is held here that has markedly pre-Christian origins. Bonfires of juniper wood, ancient symbols of

purification, are lit all the way from the top of the town down the main street to the church, and through their flames young men leap to prove their virility.

Opposite the front door of the church is the tiny town hall, incorporating the police station, of the smallest municipal capital on the island.

Hermigua

Following the road around the headland, you soon come to the broad valley of **Hermigua**, which, thanks to three streams, including the one that flows from El Cedro, has more water than anywhere else on the island and is heavily cultivated.

The narrow main road climbs through a series of villages that constitute the elongated settlement of Hermigua, passing the town hall, the post office, the church (whose earliest parts date from 1511, and which contains some finely carved altars), and a few bars and restaurants including the friendly Casa Creativa.

During the Spanish Civil War the inhabitants of this peaceful valley, along with those of Vallehermoso next door, bravely held out against Franco, and two military columns had to be sent from Tenerife to take the island by force. "Later," to quote my history book, "repression was severe."

Hermigua

Playa de la Caleta

If you take the first road to your left as you enter the valley, a very sharp left turn, it takes you behind a long and usually deserted shingle beach plagued by dangerous currents. At the far end stand the pillars that once supported the cranes that loaded the produce of Hermigua and Agulo onto ships, and below them is a swimming pool cut into the rocks that is filled by the waves.

If you turn right at the end of this road, you can drive up the left-hand side of the valley and past the cemetery before crossing over to rejoin the main road. About a kilometre after leaving the beach there is a turning to the left that will take you up over the ridge and down the other side to **Playa de la Caleta**, a very pretty sandy cove with a small restaurant serving freshly caught fish, and places to sit under the shade of trees.

Once clear of the houses of Hermigua, the newly-improved main road widens as it twists and turns, passing the road to El Cedro, and climbing steeply in its efforts to find a way through the towering walls of luxuriantly forested mountainside, which it eventually does through the 500 m Túnel de la Cumbre.

And in that short distance you leave the green and pleasant lands behind and emerge onto the arid and treeless hills above San Sebastián.

You then descend towards the capital and harbour, through three recently-cut and twisting tunnels, and fifteen uneventful kilometres later you are back where you started - at the tradesman's entrance.

Playa Santiago

TO PLAYA SANTIAGO

From Degollada de Peraza, the road to Playa Santiago descends above the village of Jerduñe, and then skirts the upper reaches of the interestingly named Barranco de Castradores (Valley of the Castrators) before cutting through a couple of tunnels and beginning its 10 km descent to the sea.

As you emerge from the tunnels, an unmade road leads off to your right. This winds down to Benchijigua and Lo del Gato, two pretty villages of scattered houses and terraces nestling below the Roque Agando in the greenest part of this barranco. Here there are many eucalyptus trees, and also many footpaths as there are six ways out of Benchijigua. In fact this whole area is splendid

Benchijigua

walking country.

Continuing down the main road, you will see signs warning you of leaping deer; but there are no deer on La Gomera, only goats; but there is no Euro-road-sign for goats. So in the interests of European conformity, if you happen to see a goat on the road, please pretend that it's a deer and don't run over it.

This is the driest part of the island, and as you zigzag down the arid Lomo de Tecina you enter Fred Olsen land, the first sight of which is a new golf course, one of the most absurd ways of wasting water ever devised by man. Below it, the low-rise and pleasantly laid out Hotel Tecina sprawls over the headland, from which you can descend to the beach via a lift-shaft cut through the cliff.

If you turn left towards the Hotel Tecina and continue past it, you come to the Playas Tapa-huga, Medio and Chinguarime, a series of stony beaches separated by headlands, and good places for snorkelling. These are by far the most pleasant beaches on this part of the coast, but they are pleasant because they are

Playa Tapahuga

unspoiled and have no facilities, so take a picnic.

When the road into Playa Santiago nears sea level, there is a turning to your left to the beach - but if you miss it don't worry, because if you turn left once you're through the tunnel you end up at the same place.

At the bend before the tunnel, a narrow road to the right leads to Pastrana and El Cabezo, and it becomes quite rural and pleasant once you get past the industrial site. The footpath beyond Pastrana will take a fit person all the way up to Los Roques.

Playa Santiago

Playa Santiago is a sleepy little fishing port and the sunniest place on the island, and it has the calmest seas. Its long, stony beach is popular with children, particularly at the harbour end, where there are breakwaters to jump off and cafés within easy reach.

The Garajonay Exprés calls in at the harbour six times a day, as it plies between Valle Gran Rey and Los Cristianos, and there are a number of picturesque fishing boats whose unloading is always fun to watch. Bar-Restaurante La Cuevita, situated in a cave below the cliffs, is an interesting place in which to eat; but otherwise the harbour is as quiet and functional as the rest of the town - a place famous for nothing much happening, particularly at night.

Leaving Playa Santiago by the other side of the valley, the first landmark you pass is the airport, rumoured to be a gift from the men in Brussels to eliminate La Gomera's qualification for third-world status. Fortunately for La Gomera, it wasn't possible to construct a runway long enough for international jets, and its declared purpose and primary function is to improve inter-island communications. Small, twin-engined aeroplanes depart daily to Tenerife and Gran Canaria, filled mainly with Gomero students attending the universities there, and of course those on serious shopping sprees.

You then climb through great swathes of abandoned terraces veined with cracked irrigation channels and dotted with palm

Playa Santiago

trees, past the villages of Anton-cojo (which means Lame Anton) and Targa, until you reach Ala-jeró, the administrative centre of this part of the island.

Alajeró's Arabic name indi-cates that it is an ancient settle-ment, and the nearby Ermita de San Isidro on the summit of Mon-taña de Calvario, to which you can walk, occupies a site where the Guanches once worshipped their sky-god Arahan. But it has no town centre as such, just a few friendly bar-restaurantes close to the church, and it is quite possible to drive through it without realising it.

Playa Santiago

2 km beyond Alajeró, a road leads off to the right around the Roque Imada to the village of Imada hidden behind it, the starting point of several walks through the upper part of the valley. 100 m further on, on the left, is a litter bin and a small lay-by, and from here a rough stone path between low walls takes you past a water tank, and then on-wards and downwards to La Gomera's one and only Dragon Tree *(Dracaena draco)*. These were once common in southern Europe, until the ice-ages drove them south, and the Canary Islands became their sole refuge.

There is no way of telling how old this tree is, because it is actually a member of the agave family and has no annual growth-rings, although several hundred years would be a conservative estimate. The Guanche kings used to hold court beneath its branches, their warriors made shields from its bark, and its thick red sap - 'dragon's blood' - was used to treat ulcers, staunch bleeding, clean teeth, strengthen gums, and was also an ingredient in their mummification process.

This dragon tree is protected by several bits of legislation, and more recently by an unsightly but necessary fence to stop visitors taking bits home.

A few hundred metres past the Dragon Tree path, a narrow road snakes off to the left to the remote and tiny village of Almá-cigos, and 1 km later you come to the Ermita de Nuestra Señora de Buen Paso, sharing its little ledge with a massive tree. Buen Paso means 'safe passage', and from here Nuestra Señora is safely carried in a festive procession every 14th September. A little way past the *ermita* another road snakes off to the left, this one leading to the hamlet of Argua-yoda 9 km away; and then, steadily reducing to a footpath, to La Rajita, where there is a deserted fish-canning factory.

These arid barrancos, now dotted with abandoned farm-houses and bits of walled-off

Dragon Tree path

The Dragon Tree

valley that were once reservoirs, were heavily cultivated less than a hundred years ago. Verdant terraces climbed from sea-level to the edge of the forest, where clouds condensed on the leaves of the trees and the water dripped and trickled through the loam to feed the nutrient-rich springs that irrigated the burgeoning crops. And with each bumper harvest another level of forest was clear-ed and new terraces were built - until, at the place where you come to a wall of pine trees and the road to Chipude, a critical point of imbalance was reached and the springs dried up never to return, leaving a stark reminder of the folly of deforestation.

Here you can either take the road to Chipude to your left [Page 58], or continue and rejoin the main road at Pajarito.

The High Plateau

TO IGUALERO, LA DAMA, CHIPUDE, EL CERCADO, LAS HAYAS & LA FORTALEZA

From Pajarito, you follow the road to Alajeró and Chipude for a couple of kilometres until you come to a fork. The left fork takes you down to Playa Santiago. The right fork leads you on a narrow winding road through the mountain villages on the 1,000 m high plateau above Valle Gran Rey, and/or down to the cliff-top village of La Dama.

The first place you pass is **Igualero**, a string of houses tucked into a narrow vale surrounded by pines and often shrouded in clouds, and at 1,300 m the highest settlement on the island. Its orange-painted church stands on a headland above the village, and beside it is a mirador with a view to La Dama.

Continuing through the forest, you arrive at a junction where you can carry on down to La Dama or turn sharp right to Chipude.

Between these roads is an unsigned and newly-laid ribbon of tarmac that leads down to the cemetery, and then continues along the ridge to the lonely village of **Gerián**, an ancient settlement where some of the houses are really caves with doors and windows. Just before

Igualero church

Farmhouse, Gerián

Cave houses, Gerián

you get to Gerián, a right fork takes you over the ridge to a tiny but beautifully situated *ermita*, one of the many on the island dedicated to the Virgin of Guadalupe. If you continue beyond the village, the road eventually terminates at Lomo de Gerián, a headland from which there is a footpath to the usually deserted Playa Iguala, where the fishing is good.

The High Plateau

If you take the La Dama road, you soon come to one of La Gomera's six filling-stations in **Apartadero**. You then pass below **La Fortaleza**, the fortress, a massive slab of lava where the last of the Guanches, for whom this was a sacred place, are said to have made their last stand against the Spaniards. A footpath from **Pavón** enables you to scramble to the top, where you feel as if you are on a giant altar to the god of the sky; as did the Guanches, and they called him Arahan.

La Dama, 15km from Chipude, is a cliff-top settlement 100m above the sea where bananas are grown in plastic greenhouses. From here a path leads down to a shingle beach and the abandoned fish factory of La Rajita, where the once-plentiful tuna were canned.

La Fortaleza

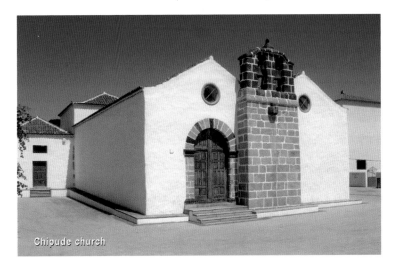

Chipude church

Turning right at the junction you enter **Chipude**, which two hundred years ago was the biggest settlement on the island. It stands 1,000 m above sea level, snowflakes have been seen to fall here, and the locals wear more clothes than anywhere else on La Gomera; but the soil is good and water plentiful, and the way of life unchanged for centuries. It is easy to drive through the centre of the village without noticing it - three bars around a plaza next to the church. Beyond it you pass the workshop of one of the longest established mechanics on the island, whose rusting sources of spare parts line the road.

The High Plateau

The next village you pass through is **El Cercado**, built in a curve at the head of the Barranco de Matanza. Here there are three **potteries** still making bowls and cooking pots from local clay in the traditional manner - that is, without a potter's wheel. You can usually watch them being made outside the shops, and once they have been taken to ancient kilns, covered with brushwood and fired, you can buy them. There are also two restaurants, María's and Victoria's, and opposite María's there is a footpath that leads down into Valle Gran Rey. [see Walks]

The last village you come to is **Las Hayas**, which means the beeches in Spain, but here it means the wax-myrtles, and they are plentiful in the woodland above the village. This is a scat-tered agricultural community on the edge of the forest above Valle Gran Rey, and a useful place to start and finish a walk; either across the rocky scrubland below the village to enjoy the views, or up through the ancient woodland of Las Creces. [see Walks]

If you turn right when you reach the junction you soon return to the main road. If you turn left you continue through Las Hayas, where from Bar Amparo, a friendly, family-run bar-restaur-ante, you can enjoy panoramic views of the village as you eat. Alternatively, a little further down the road you can eat at Bar la Montaña/Casa Efigenia, which presents the experience of a traditional Gomero meal, and is also the local shop. As well as preparing the food, Efigenia also grows most of it - but one should

bear in mind that traditional Gomeros had plenty of time and wrapped up warm.

On the edge of the cliff above Valle Gran Rey stands a cluster of radio masts, from where you can walk down a steep footpath to the village of Los Descansaderos, 500 m below, in not much longer than it takes to drive there.

Continuing beyond the village you eventually, after passing a cemetery and a series of hairpin bends, come out on the road to Valle Gran Rey just below Arure.

Valle Gran Rey

TO VALLE GRAN REY

Valle Gran Rey (the King's Great Valley) is undoubtedly the most beautiful valley on the island, and also has the best beaches and tourist facilities. And as it is to here that most visitors come, it therefore merits most attention.

From **Apartacaminos** the road winds down to a long straight stretch, which passes a short circular walk through the trees, Los Barranquillos, and takes you out of the forest. At the end of the straight stretch the **Mirador de Alojera** is to your right, where a gravelled track takes you to a

stone platform, from which you look down from the top of the Lomo del Carretón over the coastal village of Alojera with the island of La Palma on the horizon.

Continuing downhill, you pass through **Arure**, once the seat of the kings of Valle Gran Rey, a long straggling village along a fertile valley of deep-red earth. Here the large Bar-Restaurante Conchita serves traditional Gomero food that has won prizes. At the bottom of the village is the **Mirador de Santo**, where you climb the steps and walk under

Valle Gran Rey from
La Curva de Queso

the archway for a view over the scattered village of Taguluche, from a platform that you share with a small chapel. If you follow the footpath to the right you can walk there - it's getting back that's the problem.

The road then crosses the valley, and cuts along the almost vertical side of the Barranco de Arure before passing through a tunnel, after which you come to the Restaurante/Mirador de Caesár Manrique. **Caesár Manrique** was a celebrated Canarian architect and painter, and his speciality was designing buildings that blended with the landscape. This one certainly blends from above - you would never guess that underneath those unassuming mounds of stone and winding paths lies a massive restaurant with a great curved window and panoramic views. But from the villages below, particularly at night, it looks as if an alien spaceship has landed on the valley rim. From its flat roof you look down on the horseshoe of villages in the upper part of Valle Gran Rey, which is called **Guadá**.

A little way beyond the mirador the road almost makes a 360°

turn at **La Curva de Queso**, the cheese curve, so called because of its round shape. Here there is a large lay-by from which you can look down on the lower part of Valle Gran Rey - the village half-way down the valley is El Guro, and on the coast you can see the houses and beach of La Puntilla.

The road then descends steeply, doubles back, tunnels through the mountain below the Curva de Queso, and emerges into **Valle Gran Rey**.

Restaurante/Mirador de Caesár Manrique

Valle Gran Rey

The first building you encounter, at the second bend, is the church of San Antonio, and at the third bend there is a turning to the left to Lomo del Balo and the other villages on the far side of **Guadá**. This narrow and tricky road is best done on foot, and there is a detailed guide in the Walks section.

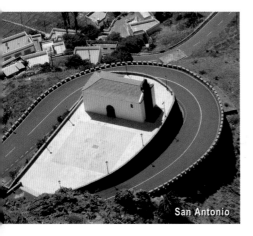

San Antonio

You then pass through the upper part of Retamal, out past the café-like Tanatorio Municipal (Municipal Mortuary), back past the cemetery, and through the lower part of Retamal via the last hairpin bend before the sea.

From here on it's only tight curves; and after winding through Lomo del Moral and Los Granados, you reach a three-lane straightish stretch down to Casa de la Seda and El Guro.

These adjacent villages stand either side of the mouth of the Barranco de Arure, the top of which you drove round before entering the first tunnel; and if you walk up it for a couple of kilometres you come to a small waterfall. [see Walks]

A little further on there is a right fork leading up to the **Centro Medico** and Las Orijamas, while the new road takes you down to **La Calera**, the administrative centre of Valle Gran Rey. Here the Ayuntamiento (town hall), Centro Cultural, petrol station, taxi rank, a few bars and cafés, and the church are clustered where the road divides. Behind them, stepped and winding paths take you through this small and almost vertical town built up the side of a cliff, where there are a number of restaurants and boutiques, a language school, a few supermarkets, and many apartments for rent.

La Calera stands at the apex of the fertile delta that fills the wide mouth of Valle Gran Rey,

Poinsettia

and at the roundabout you have the choice of Puerto to your left or Playa to your right. The triangle is completed by the coast road that runs between them.

Cemetery

La Calera

TO PUERTO

The *puerto* (harbour) is called **Vueltas**, and on your way there, on the left, you pass the large and long-established El Palmar Restaurante where there is often live music, the two main banks (BBVA and La Caixa), the post office (Correos) (up a side street in Borbalán), a Swiss café/ bakery, and the Chinese restaurant.

The road through **Vueltas** is one-way from the other end, and it is easiest to turn left at the roundabout, park and walk. The narrow and mostly pedestrian streets of this bustling and compact fishing village are crammed with shops of every description - boutiques, Internet, healthfood, African art, car and motorbike rental, ironmongers, an excellent German butcher facing the sea, a fitness studio, five supermarkets, a disco, and Capitano Claudio, who trades in things nautical, including whale-watching and fishing excursions in small boats.

There are several good restaurants, notably Bar Puerto for its fish, El Pescador for its chicken, and Tambara for Moroccan and Habibi for Arabian cuisine; Chiquitin makes the best and fastest pizzas on the island, and a place to sit over a *café con leche* is never far away.

Of the many bars, Bar Puerto is the oldest and the most 'local', La Cacatua the liveliest and most informal, and Bar Tasca is a popular cocktail bar with ingenious décor. The biggest building in the village is the banana co-operative, where you can watch, from a distance, bananas being trimmed and weighed and packed into boxes.

The **Garajonay Exprés** leaves the harbour three times a day for Los Cristianos via Santiago and San Sebastián, and the ticket office is on the quay. But unfortunately, as I write, and certainly for the next few years, the harbour and its environs have become a massive building site. It is being more than doubled in size, transformed into a car-ferry port with a marina for 300 boats and a boatyard, etc. And although the calm harbour beach has so far remained unscathed, apart from heavy lorries thundering behind it, and although the café on the quay is still a pleasant place to sit and look at the boats, in the current conditions the best

thing to do here is head for the open ocean. [see Excursion Boats]

The other way to escape the dust and din of the harbour is to follow the path below the cliffs to the smooth stones of **Playa Argaga**. From here a demanding but exciting footpath marked by red dots on the rocks will take you up the barranco to Gerián and beyond. Behind the beach is the Finca Argayall, a German enlightenment centre where they grow organic fruit & veg, and where you can discuss the esoteric and meditate for a small contribution.

If you climb over the rocks at the far end you come to **Playa de las Arenas**, known locally as the Pig Beach and home to an ad hoc tribe of New Age troglodytes, but peaceful and usually sandy.

Valle Gran Rey

PUERTO TO PLAYA

If you follow the coast road north-wards from the roundabout at Vueltas, you soon come to **El Charco del Conde** (The Count's Pool), often called the Baby Beach; one of the treasures of Valle Gran Rey and a *Site of Scientific Interest*. This is a shallow lagoon with a wide, sandy and always calm beach fringed with thickets of tamarisk, and protected from the waves by a broad band of rocks.

Across the road is the reliable Bar-Restaurante Charco del Conde, that started life in a shack beside the lagoon until a storm washed it away. Also across the road, and down the steps, are an Italian ice-cream parlour and Los Girasoles, a Belgian restaurant.

Continuing along the coast road you come to **La Puntilla**, where Bike Station Gomera can rent you a bicycle and offer you transport to the top of the island for a downhill run. There are also a few shops, restaurants, the Hotel Gran Rey, and the friendly Bar El Eden tucked around the corner. And stretching away be-fore you is 500 m of beach divided by the mouth of the bar-ranco, with all the amenities of La

Playa at the far end.

The island you can see on the horizon is El Hierro.

El Charco del Conde

La Playa

Valle Gran Rey

TO PLAYA

If, at the roundabout in La Calera, you turn right for Playa, you pass a small Artesanía de Piel (leather workshop) on your right. Here Domingo and Oscar will pause

their cobbling to measure you up for sturdy shoes and sandals, or serve you a pair they prepared earlier, or a belt or a bag.

Just past their workshop, until very recently, the newly-constructed road narrowed because an electricity pylon stood in one of the lanes. The pylon was there first by many years, but these sort of things happen on La Gomera.

This end of the beach and the surrounding area is officially called La Playa de la Calera, but it is normally referred to as **Playa María**, and Bar Jornadas on the corner of the road as Casa María.

Here the venerable María, now past eighty, still keeps an eye on things. Her bar-restaurante has been the focus of Playa life since long before tourism; it was once also the post-office and general store, and later the first pension; and it remains the best place to watch the winter sunsets.

To the left of María's is the pleasant terrace of Casa de la Playa, and to its right, beyond the little plaza and shed-sized Ermita de San Pedro, is the promenade with many open-air restaurants from which to enjoy a panoramic view of the beaches. Here also, in a cellar, is the disco.

In the streets behind the promenade you will find the Tourist Information Office, an Internet café, Fisch & Co the diving school, a large supermarket that doesn't take siesta, and several bars and restaurants. Notable among the bars are La Tasca, a pub-like bar run by an Englishman, the large and cheerful tapas bar Casa Pancho, and the elegant Café Étnico. In the middle street is El Baifo, probably the best restaurant on La Gomera, where the predominantly Malaysian food is all cooked by the cheery owner Ng Yee Thoong, better known as Andy.

Valle Gran Rey

PLAYA DEL INGLÉS

If you continue northwards beyond Playa, past the apartment blocks, and follow the unmade road, you arrive at the unspoiled Playa del Inglés, another of the treasures of Valle Gran Rey. This is a protected area, and beyond the rocks and dunes to your left is the Charco de Cieno, known locally as **Charco de la Bruja** (the witch's pool), a tidal pond frequented by curlews, whimbrils and godwits, and another *Site of Scientific Interest*.

Playa del Inglés itself is part of the Parque Rural de Valle Gran Rey, so there are no disfiguring amenities other than a litter bin, and when there is sand this is the most beautiful beach on La Gomera. But it is also the most dangerous when the waves are big, and here the warnings on page 198 should be most rigorously heeded.

It lies at the foot of **La Mérica**, a 600 m cliff of volcanic strata above which clouds often condense. And while it's not officially a nudist beach, it's not necessary to dress up to sunbathe or swim if you don't want to, and many people don't.

From here El Hierro is on the horizon to your left, and the twin peaks of La Palma to your right.

Alojera

TO ALOJERA, TAGULUCHE, ARGUAMUL, TAZO & EPINA

A little way past the Chorros de Epina, an unassuming turn-off to the left, signposted Arguamul, Taguluche, Epina, Alojera and Tazo, provides the only access to about one tenth of La Gomera.

This is a sparsely populated and very much unspoiled area that lies at the foot of a magnificent backdrop, the Monumento Natural del Lomo del Carretón, a 5 km long wall of cliffs speckled with pine trees that rises to 1 km above sea level.

The two main villages, Alojera and Taguluche, are less than 3 km apart as the crow flies, but they are separated by a high, pinnacled ridge, and connected by 14 km of long and winding road. This whole area is worthy of at least a day's exploration.

Lomo del Carretón

Arguamul

500 m after leaving the main road, there is a hairpin bend, where an unmade road turns off to the right, signposted Tazo and Arguamul. This is quite driveable, and forks after 1 km.

The left fork takes you past the extensive village of Tazo, famed for its *miel de palma*, before turning to lead you down through it and on to Alojera. As it makes the turn, a surprisingly asphalted road appears on your right which takes you safely round the mountain to Arguamul, the most remote and reputedly the windiest settlement on the island. Below it, a remarkable series of asphalted zigzags lead

you to the clifftop houses of Guillama.

The right fork takes you, with views and precipices to your left, to the lonely Ermita de Santa Clara. It then crosses to the other side of the ridge, where the valleys and villages of Vallehermoso appear a long way below you with Tenerife looming in the background, and continues past the even more lonely Ermita de Nuestra Señora de Coromoto; until, 4 km after you forked, you drive up a long ramp to Punta de Alcalá - a windswept platform 564 m above the sea, with a view well worth the effort of getting there.

Alojera

Continuing along the road to Alojera, you pass above the village of Epina and below a brace of wind-generators, and then swing round to the left; and 2 km later the road to Taguluche heads off to the left. This winds its way along the base of the Lomo del Carretón, and between the pinnacles of the dividing ridge, before the village comes into view. It then plunges, via a series of tight hairpin bends, among the scattered houses of this cliff-top agricultural settlement until it can go no further, after which further progress is by foot; but only as far as the tops of the cliffs. The path used to lead all the way to the sea, down it donkeys carried the produce of Taguluche to be loaded onto ships, but much of it has now fallen away, and only the concrete pillars that once supported a crane remain of the harbour.

There is a small beach to the north of Taguluche, Playa de Guariñén, that can be reached by a steep and tricky zigzag track from the church, which stands 200 m above it.

Taguluche from Lomo del Carretón

Playa de Alojera

From the Taguluche turn-off, the road to Alojera descends through what is almost a forest of palm trees as it heads for the sea, and eventually, after winding its way through the scattered village, it almost gets there. You are left with a short walk through the steep, stepped streets of a small fishing village to a usually sandy and rarely busy beach. This is protected by a breakwater from which you can fish and splash, and the submerged part of the breakwater is a favourite place for scuba divers. There are two pleasant restaurants and plenty of apartments, some along the seafront, making Playa de Alojera the perfect place for an extremely quiet holiday.

Parque Nacional

PARQUE NACIONAL DE GARAJONAY

There are sixteen legally protected natural sites on La Gomera. Fifteen of them are theoretically protected by local laws, but the Parque Nacional de Garajonay, 3,984 hectares of subtropical rainforest covering the mountainous centre of La Gomera, has the protection of the UN and is secure for future generations to enjoy. In 1986, UNESCO declared it a World Heritage Site, and now Medio Ambiente, the environment people, tend it with great care - mostly by simply leaving it alone and encouraging others to do the same.

It is thought to be the last surviving tract of the sort of forest that covered the lands around the Mediterranean until about two million years ago. Then the ice-ages, and the desertification of North Africa, eliminated it from everywhere except the western Canary Islands - until about five hundred years ago, when man set about completing the task.

But the real point about the Parque Nacional de Garajonay is that it is pristine primeval woodland; woodland as it was before civilisation appeared; woodland that has been spared acid rain and logging; woodland of the sort that has all but disappeared in the rest of the world. The close-packed trunks form impenetrable barriers, dead trees lean in the arms of their offspring, spindly young saplings stretch for the gaps in the canopy, mosses drape trunks and branches with a deep and vibrant green, yellow lichens hang like beards, ferns and other undergrowth thrive in the rich loam, butterflies dance in the patches of sunlight, and when the wind blows you are enveloped in a cacophony of soughing and creaking and the knocking of wood on wood.

Parque Nacional

The predominant tree, certainly around the edges of the forest, is the heather-tree *(Erica arborea)*, known locally as *brezo*. Its flowers crown the island with lucky white heather in the springtime, and its tiny leaves are particularly good at condensing water from passing clouds. They usually grow in close association with the Canary wax-myrtle *(Myrica faya)*, creating a type of forest known as 'fayal-brezal', which covers most of the southern slopes.

The other dominant trees, especially around El Cedro on the humid northern slopes, are Canary laurel *(Laurus azorica)* and Canary holly *(Ilex canarienses)*, and this type of forest is known as 'laurisilva'.

Varying combinations of these trees, interspersed with sometimes quite extensive stands of Canary pine *(Pinus canariensis)*, constitute the bulk of the woodland in the Parque Nacional. There are, of course, a great many other sorts of trees mixed among them, including palm trees, along with a huge supporting cast of shrubs, ferns, herbs, flowers, etc.

Fire is as great a threat to the survival of this ancient forest as man, and many of the old tracks have been widened to accommodate fire-engines, while the trees and brush beside them are regularly thinned to create firebreaks. You are not allowed to drive along these forestry roads, but they do provide easy strolling and are usually well signposted. Many ancient footpaths are also kept clear, enabling you to penetrate deep into the woodland. [see Walks]

Four barbecue areas have been created in the Parque Nacional; at La Laguna Grande, Las Creces, Los Chorros de Epina and La Ermita de las Nieves. They all have stone ovens, firewood, springwater, and rustic tables and benches; and they are there to be used, and left as you found them.

Walking

Advice

La Gomera has been thoroughly walked for centuries, and there are more than enough well-trodden footpaths on which to get safely lost without wandering deep into virgin forest or over the tops of precipices. In most cases the footpaths take not only the most direct route, but also the only safe route. Goats, however, can create deceptive paths, and the paths that are simply for access to cultivated terraces can lead you astray. But as long as you stick to the obvious paths, and remember your way back, you can't go far wrong.

It is always a sensible precaution when heading off into the wilderness to wear something white or of a bright colour in case a helicopter needs to find you, and also to carry a small torch, a knife, a bottle of water, a bag of nuts and a bar of chocolate. The best chocolate for the purpose is La Candelaria, unsophisticated and locally made, with a high melting-point, because refined chocolate liquefies soon after sun-up. And it's very important in this cactus-rich land to carry a pair of tweezers; and also something wind- and water-proof.

For those who enjoy serious hiking, I strongly recommend that you find an experienced guide. They know the best walks, how long they take, and their degrees of difficulty; they know the effects of the climate and terrain; and most importantly they know how to get back to where you are staying at the end of the day. Advertisements for their services can be found in shop-windows and on café noticeboards. There are also several hiking guide-books [see Further Reading], and the best are in German; but none are by people who live here, and all can be quite misleading.

Suggestions for walks are scattered throughout the Tour Round the Island. The following selection are for those who, like myself, prefer an extended and mildly adventurous stroll through beautiful surroundings. They can all be done in two to three hours; but with a break for a picnic, and pauses to enjoy the views and the peace and quiet, they can be made to last all day.

The Waterfall, Valle Gran Rey

TO THE WATERFALL IN EL BARRANCO DE ARURE, VALLE GRAN REY

To reach this waterfall requires quite a bit of clambering and scrambling and ducking under branches. Hands, knees, and at times bottoms will be needed, and feet will probably get wet. But there are no obstacles that should unduly tax the resources of an averagely fit person, and children find it great fun.

Your objective lies at the end of a narrow and verdant ravine, El Barranco de Arure, which climbs gently behind the villages of El Guro and Casa de la Seda,

which lie either side of the stream that runs down the ravine. The waterfall is about 2 km from the road, and you should be able to get there and back at an easy pace within three hours.

You park, or alight from the bus, or get your bearings, in Casa de la Seda, which is about 20 mins walk from La Calera. The walk begins on the left-hand side of the road facing uphill, across from the upper parking spaces, where there is a footpath beside a palm tree with *Wasserfall* painted on its trunk and a sign that says 'El Guro'.

El Guro actually starts when you cross the stream at the bottom of the slope, and you follow the steps up through the village until you come to a couple of triangular windows on your right. At the second of these you turn sharply right and see a sign for 'cascada', which is Spanish for *Wasserfall*.

The path now becomes more rustic, and level, and as you leave the houses the valley appears before you. For a while the path slopes downwards, until it more or less follows the course

El Guanche

of a large water-pipe below a wall of lava columns, and a little way past El Guanche you reach what looks like a large can on a stick fixed to the top of the pipe. Here the path climbs to the left between prickly pear cacti, its course marked with yellow and blue flags and roundels painted on the rocks. Below you are palms and fruit trees, and it should go without saying that you stay off cultivated terraces and don't nick the fruit.

After a while the prickly pear cacti thin, and are replaced by candelabra-like stands of Canary spurge, between which aloe vera covers the ground. You continue until another valley opens to your left, where the path slopes steeply down towards the stream, deteriorating into a fall of boulders before you reach the bottom.

From here on it is simplest to follow the course of the stream, which is shaded and cool and picturesque, and really what this walk is all about. Many paths lead up from the stream and can be fun to explore, but they're mostly for access to terraces, or to

bypass bits of the stream that become impassable after heavy rain. The level of the water when it is in flood can be gauged by the tangles of dried vegetation caught in the trees and cane, often well above head height. Several times you will have to scramble up the sides of small waterfalls, where the wet rocks, as you would expect, are slippery - and remember that wet shoes on dry rocks are equally slippery, and the cause of many painful experiences.

All the while the ravine steadily narrows and becomes more full of trees, until quite suddenly you reach the end - a small cove of high lava cliffs where grey wagtails nest, down which the waterfall tumbles. Not quite Niagara, but the best La Gomera has to offer, and a very welcome shady place to splash and drink and cool off before retracing your steps.

You return along the stream until you reach the place where you joined it - where you will see 'El Guro' painted on a boulder. To avoid scrambling up again, continue along the stream bed until a wooden structure appears on your right. Then follow the water pipe for a short while until a rough path climbs to your left. Take this path, and you will soon be among the houses of Casa de la Seda (The House of Silk), where you rejoin the road about 50 m above where your walk began.

Canary spurge

Walking

Arure to
Valle Gran Rey

Take the steps to the right

Goat cave

ARURE TO LA CALERA VIA LA MÉRICA

First get to Arure; either by bus to Bar Jape, or cadge a lift. The walk starts at the bottom of Arure at the turn-off to the Mirador de Santo.

You follow this road past the mirador and a line of houses, where it turns right and becomes a dirt road. This takes you around a rocky outcrop, where Taguluche lies a long way below you to your right, 700 m more or less - there is a track off to the right that will lead you down there.

You continue past a collection of beehives in caves to your left, from where you will probably see smoke rising from a barranco away to your right. This is the Barranco de Basura, the municipal rubbish dump, where the contents of Valle Gran Rey's wheely-bins are tipped and ignited.

There are a great many free-range goats in this area, some wearing bells so they can be found for milking - they do nothing more than bleat and look at you. The occasional donkey, on the other hand, is tethered,

Arure

and while they are normally docile, I've known them bite and kick and I always check the length of their rope as I pass them by.

The dirt road is there for the rubbish trucks, and not far past the dump a stepped path leads up to the right where VGR ➘ is painted on a rock. This heads for the top of the line of trees ahead, where it turns right and continues along the ridge through aromatic pines.

Across the valley you can see the road into Valle Gran Rey snaking round the Curva de Queso and through the tunnel; Vueltas becomes visible in the mouth of the valley; the church of Los Reyes appears below you; and above the opposite side of

the valley from left to right are the villages of Las Hayas, El Cercado, Chipude and the lava slab of La Fortaleza.

After climbing a few zigzags you pass a goat pen, and then a large and partly-walled cave that has long been used for accommodating goats, which you can usually smell well before you get there.

A little further on you reach the highest point, and before you lies the great sloping plateau of La Mérica, covered with abandoned terraces. On the far side of the rocky outcrop to your left stand the ruins of the old farmhouse, once a beautiful house of lava and red tosca; and in the middle of the plateau are the ruins of the farm buildings, past

The road into Valle Gran Rey rounds the Curva de Queso and tunnels below it

Walking

Arure to Valle Gran Rey

Ancient lava flow

The path across La Mérica

The ruined farmhouse

which the path runs.

If you continue to the end of the headland, you can look down on Playa del Inglés half a kilometre below you, and it is from here that hang-gliders leap. Your path down to La Calera leads off to the left shortly before you get to the end, at what can seem a confusing junction, but I can assure you that there is only the one path.

From this point onwards the views of the delta of Valle Gran Rey are breathtaking - and it is best to stop walking before admiring them. This ancient zigzagging trackway is constructed in the same way that it has been for centuries, with handy rocks and stones wedged together and packed with grit, and it should be trodden with great care.

It's 500 m from the top to the bottom, during which you cover 500 m horizontally; and it seems to go on for ever and you will probably feel a profound sense of relief when you finally reach the gently sloping tarmac in Las Orijamas.

Here you turn right, and a further ten minutes of walking on jelly legs will bring you to the comforts of La Calera.

The delta of Valle Gran Rey

El Cercado to Valle Gran Rey

EL CERCADO TO LA VIZCAÍNA

The bus will take you up to El Cercado, where this short and spectacular walk starts at Bar María. El Cercado is a pretty village built around the top of one of the barrancos that create Valle Gran Rey, and it boasts three traditional potteries which should be visited before you head downhill. Bar María is situated at one end of the village, and is quite unmistakable - it is mauve, inside and out, and around the crowded walls of the bar are narrow shelves bearing hundreds of lighters, key-rings and miniatures, and supporting some remarkable hanging plants.

Opposite the door of Bar María is a narrow road leading between the houses. You follow this alongside a green railing, the road quickly becomes unmade, and as you near the crest you take the footpath which branches off to your right.

These are the only instructions you need, as this is the only path; and a very ancient track it is too. It's wide enough for a laden donkey, and for most of its length it consists of stones packed together; which is fine for a

donkey, but if you've only got two legs you will need to tread carefully, and I would advise you to stop walking before admiring the views.

Immediately to your right, and a long way below you, is the ravine of the Barranco de Agua; ahead are the villages of Guadá at the top of Valle Gran Rey, your destination; and towering above you to your left are outcrops of lava speckled with lichen and dotted with houseleeks. Water leaks out of the mountainside in two or three places along the path, where with patience you can fill a cup; but these springs make the path slippery. Growing beside the path are what looks like a large-leafed sage: this is Valle Gran Rey False Sage

The start of the footpath

(Sideritis nutans), one of three species of false sage exclusive to La Gomera.

Valle Gran Rey false sage

The path descends relatively gently, with steep bits, until you are almost directly above La Vizcaína. Then it zigzags down the ridge to the houses, and before you know it you're standing on the road thinking - 'That was quick!' The locals reckon it takes an hour, although they don't pause to admire the views and take photos, but unless you stop for a picnic you should complete this descent from 1,000 m to 400 m in 90 minutes.

You are now on the Walk Around Guadá - the next walk. If you turn left, you can soon refresh yourself at Bar-Bodegón La Vizcaína, and another hour of gentle downhill strolling will take you to La Calera.

The footpath

Around Guadá, Valle Gran Rey

A WALK AROUND GUADÁ, VALLE GRAN REY

Guadá is the upper part of Valle Gran Rey, and it consists of a horseshoe of nine villages built along the ridges between the cliffs and the valley floor, where they are safe from the rockfalls and torrents of the winter storms.

Three of these villages lie on the main road, the remainder are served by a loop of single-track road from which steep stepped paths lead up and down to the houses. Some of the upward paths continue all the way to the tops of the cliffs and the villages out of sight over the rim. The downward paths head for the three or four places where you can usually cross the stream, and some vanish before reaching it and reappear on the other side.

This great bowl of villages and terraces is a very pleasant place for simply wandering around and exploring, full of surprises and visual delights, and almost impossible to get lost in. Although you may have to backtrack from time to time, as there is often no way to distinguish between the public footpaths and paths leading to houses or goat-sheds, until you encounter a gate or a goat.

You can start this walk in La Calera, from where it's more interesting to take the old road to your left, or the one above it, than the new bypass - they all meet up again just below the Centro Medico. Once past El Guro and Casa de la Seda, there is an arduous three-lane stretch that ascends through the narrowest part of the valley. The climate often changes along this stretch, and the weather in the lower and upper valley can be distinctly different.

Guadá begins where the third lane ends, and the first village is Los Granados. Here you pass a supermarket, a bus stop, and a road that leads across to the other side of the valley. If you've come this far by car, this is a useful place to park and start walking.

From Los Granados, you follow the main road around the end of the ridge, past the police station (Guardia Civil), and through Lomo del Moral, until you come to a telephone box, a bus stop (El Colegio) and a hairpin bend. In front of you is a footpath that takes you past the school and over the stream, and then forks to either side of the valley. These forks further divide and subdivide as they lead, always upwards, to the surrounding villages, and ultimately to the road that this walk follows. Conversely, if you descend from the road by any footpath this is where you usually end up.

A few metres past the hairpin bend, take the road that cuts back to your right. This is the last remaining bit of the old road into Valle Gran Rey, a series of steep zigzags that take you up through Retamal and back to the main road; where you turn right and soon come to Bar Retamal, the first bar after La Calera.

Walking
Around Guadá, Valle Gran Rey

At the next hairpin bend, where there is another bus stop (Lomo del Balo), take the road to your right. This is the highest point in Guadá, where you leave the traffic behind, and where the strictly downhill strollers can begin this walk.

You first cross a bridge over a narrow ravine, and ahead of you to your left is the Barranco de Las Hayas, one of the two valleys that combine to become Valle Gran Rey. A rough footpath to your left where the road turns right will take you up to Las Hayas, but you'll need a head for heights as part of it is along a precipice.

The road then takes you through Lomo del Balo, and past Bar Lomo del Balo, which has a view that makes you back away

Harvesting yams

from the window. Most of the village is above or below you, and as you round the *lomo*, which means ridge, the path down from the corner is particularly pretty. If you follow it until you come to a water tank, and there turn left, it becomes a narrow track through the *caña* as it crosses the stream, and then winds up past terraces to the road.

From Lomo del Balo, the road slopes gently to Los Descansaderos at the mouth of the verdant Barranco de Agua, the other

Lomo del Balo

valley that becomes Valle Gran Rey.

Guadá is a contraction of *aguada,* which means 'the watering-place', Los Descansaderos means 'the resting places', the water that trickles out of the cliffs on the right of the Barranco de Agua flows all the year round, and in times of drought Gomeros and their livestock came down from the high pastures to congregate around this oasis. I've been told that a hundred years ago the stream ran all the way down the

valley to the sea and that eels were caught in it, and even today it provides most of the water for Valle Gran Rey.

There is a path that climbs the ridge from here to the radio masts at the top of the cliff, and if you walk up until you come to the irrigation channel, and then follow it to the right, you soon find your-self among lush greenery and tumbling waters.

Once the road has crossed the stream it turns right, and after a short rise begins its long descent towards the sea. You are now passing through La Vizcaína, and next to the telephone-box is a path that will take you above the Barranco de Agua to El Cercado.

Barranco de Agua

[see previous Walk] The next path to the left, 100 m further on, takes you over the top to the next valley and the village of Gerián; and at the next bend stands Bar Bodegón La Vizcaína, where you can eat and drink and enjoy the views from the balcony.

From here you descend quite steeply through Higuera de Llano, which blends into the old village of El Hornillo, where the road squeezes its way between close-packed houses and is in places the width of a laden donkey. At the bottom of El Hornillo there is a sharp bend, where you have the choice of following the road down to the bridge and up the other side to Los Granados and the main road (where you may have parked), or of turning left and continuing down this side of the valley to La Calera.

If you turn left, in a short while you come to Chelé, the last village in Guadá, and here the road stops and you continue your descent by footpath. For a short while it is paved and takes you past a house built onto a cave, but at the next house the paved bit descends to another house, and you continue along the old track. Very old in fact, and until

very recently all the footpaths were like this and the roads were not much better.

At the next barranco on your left stands a small house, and the track beside it leads up and over the top to Gerián: and after passing the next barranco, which has a wall built across it to catch falling rocks, you come to La Ermita de los Reyes. This small church perches on a high ledge, and below it is Burro Parque, a donkey sanctuary and stables where you can go riding.

Just past the church, the footpath zigzags down to cross the valley floor and join the main road. But if at the first bend you take the narrow and often overgrown path to your left, this will lead you gently down, with a small scramble at the end, to the floor of the barranco. And from there a broad dirt road takes you past the council's works-department to La Calera, where you can clamber up to the road, or continue until you get to the steps by the bridge.

LAS CRECES

Creces are the fruit of the wax-myrtle (Myrica faya), the dominant tree in this part of the forest, and they cover the forest floor in the autumn. They look like pea-sized blackberries, are quite dry with a nutty taste, and have a hard pip in the middle; and they formed an important part of the Guanche diet.

Creces

This walk starts at the main road, where there is a sign between the turn-offs to Las Hayas and Valle Gran Rey. It begins with 700 m of forestry road that leads you deep into the woodland to the clearing called Las Creces. Here there are barbecue ovens, rustic tables and benches, and springwater from a tap.

In the days before Las Creces became part of the Parque Nacional, and the spring was piped off to Arure, goatherds gathered their flocks here at night, and their munching of saplings created this open space. But as goats eventually destroy forests by eating all the new trees, they are now banned.

Around this clearing stand ancient wax-myrtles, the old trunks surrounded by new shoots which will eventually replace them, a system of regeneration that enables these trees to survive fire, drought and goats. Between them, in winter and spring, the ground is carpeted pink with Canary cranesbill; and in the early summer, when the trees are in blossom, the canopy hums with the buzzing of millions of bees.

From the clearing you take the path beside the heather-tree, which stands beside the notice-board and a wooden post. This post once had a '1' painted on it, and is one of eleven along this trail that go with an educational 'self guider' booklet that is now very difficult to obtain.

This narrow path leads you through some of the most beautiful and luxuriant woodland on La

Las Creces

Gomera, and for the first few hundred metres you walk beside a line of half-buried stones that once formed a channel to carry the water from the spring to Arure. Little sunlight reaches the forest floor, so the soil remains damp and the air humid. Giant ferns make the most of the light that does break through, yellow lichen thrive in the humidity and festoon the branches, and quite huge fungi grow from the trunks.

Where a tree has fallen, the resulting patch of sunlight is soon colonised by a variety of small plants, including Balm of Gilead *(Cedronella canariensis)*, several kinds of mint, thyme, Canary cistus from which you can brew a relief for toothache, and the ubiquitous Canary cranesbill. These clearings are also good places for finding wildlife, such as the wingless cricket, cleopatra and red admiral butterflies, and laurel pigeons, to name but a few.

When you reach post N°5 you are in the presence of a 'ghost tree'. This is the Canary Holly or *aceviño (Ilex canariensis)*, easily recognised by the beards of moss that cover its light coloured bark, which give it a ghostly appearance in the mist. It pro-

duces red berries, but doesn't have the prickly leaves of European holly.

At post N°6 are young Canary Laurel trees *(Laurus azorica)*, a sign of the recovery of this part of the forest. They were once scarce, as their leaves were used to feed goats and their trunks were the first choice for roof beams.

A little way past this post a path leads off to Arure, and here you bear left and climb gently

Beefsteak fungus

Balm of Gilead

along the side of another small valley, and then up a series of steps made with logs, until you come to a crossroads with the forestry road. If you carry straight on you come to the church of Las Hayas, from where, if you turn right at the road, you soon come to Bar-Restaurante Amparo. Turning right on the forestry road will bring you to the lower part of Las Hayas, and if you turn left you will return to the clearing where you started.

CAÑADA DE JORGE

The other signposted walk from this stretch of road, the nearby Cañada de Jorge (George's gully), is also a very pleasant stroll through equally beautiful but subtly different woodland.

There are two starting points on the road about 600 m apart, and the path loops between them. It also has a turn-off to Arure that joins up with the path from Las Creces.

Lichen

El Cedro

EL CEDRO

The laurel forest of El Cedro is an extensive walking area of exceptional natural beauty, and has a great many footpaths and a stream that flows all year round.

The purpose of this particular walk is to follow the stream down through the laurel trees to the *caserío* (hamlet) of El Cedro, and then climb up the side of the valley and return through heather-trees and wax-myrtle; and also to introduce you to the area and whet your appetite for further exploration.

The road to El Cedro turns off the road from Los Roques to Hermigua about 2 km from the top, and you follow this narrow crazy-paved road, whose loose stones rattle beneath your wheels, for 3 km into the heart of the forest. Your destination is El Arroyo (the stream) at a place called Las Mimbreras (the wickerworkers), and the only turn-off is the road to El Caserío, which soon leaves the forest and becomes unattractively functional. Beyond this junction your road loses its clattering stones and becomes the old earth road to Los Aceviños.

You park at Las Mimbreras, and take the footpath signed Ermita and Caserío de El Cedro, which more or less follows the course of the stream. After a few hundred metres you cross a small bridge, and a chapel dedicated to the Virgin of Lourdes appears between the trees. This was erected at the behest of an English lady, Florence Parry, who died in 1964. Close by its paved forecourt you can enjoy a drink of fresh water from a tree, because, by a novel bit of ingenious whimsy, a spring has been piped up its trunk and pours forth from a hollow branch at head height.

You continue down the valley beneath the high canopy of the laurel trees, with the stream gurgling constantly to your left, until picturesque small houses nestling in their clearings start to appear. Here patches of pink lilies sprout leafless from the earth attracting orange and yellow cleopatra butterflies *(Gonepteryx cleobule)*, ancient sweet chestnut trees overhang the path, and terraces of apple trees step down towards the stream.

Then the path slowly widens, more houses come into view, you leave the protection of the

El Cedro

Parque Nacional and it shows, and you see signs for Bar La Vista. Here you can pause for refreshment and decide whether to return the way you came, or to climb up the other side of the valley.

From behind Bar La Vista a dirt road leads upwards, which you follow almost to the Casa Rural, and then fork right along a narrow track that leads you back into the trees. To your right you can see down the barranco to Hermigua, and for what seems like a long time the path climbs steeply and its general direction seems like the wrong one, until, just as you're about to give up, you emerge on a dirt road. Here you turn left, the hardest bit behind you, and a little further on you turn left again - the valley should be below you to your left.

This road, the only road, will lead you back to your car. For about a kilometre it follows the 1,000 m contour line, and then slowly descends in a series of long zigzags, until you hear the sound of the stream below you and in a short while you are back where you started.

The path that leads upstream from here is equally beautiful, and will take you, in 4.5 km and via many steps, to the top of Garajonay. But it is more enjoyable to start there and walk down to Las Mimbreras, where your driver can prepare a picnic and await you on the banks of the stream.

Garajonay

SUNSET & MOONLIGHT ON GARAJONAY

This is one of the most effortless and magical walks on La Gomera. The objectives are a gentle stroll through a beautiful forest to watch the sun sink into the ocean from the top of the mountain, followed by a gentle stroll back to your car by the light of an almost-full moon. But to achieve this requires careful planning, as it can only be done in the four days before a full moon. The best day is two days before full-moon, and its success depends on reasonably clear skies.

The full effects of this excursion can be achieved with a little over 3 km of walking along an almost level forestry road, and even if you continue all the way to the top of Garajonay, you ascend less than 100 m in 3.4 km, with most of that at the end. The only warning is to take something warm to put on, as at 1,400 m above sea level it can get very chilly when the sun goes down.

If you can't arrange your visit to tie in with a full moon, don't let that put you off, as the views from the mountaintop and the beauty of the forest make this walk an extremely rewarding way to pass a few hours at any time of day.

You first drive to the junction of the main road and the road to Alajeró and Chipude - a place called Pajarito, although you won't know that until you come to the first signpost pointing the way you've come. You should arrive at least an hour before sunset.

The walk starts on the opposite side of the junction to the

parking place - a forestry road with a chain across it. A signpost visible at the far end points to Alto de Garajonay 2.5 km - a short-cut to the top, which you ignore. Instead, follow the forestry road, whose overall direction, after rounding the end of a valley, is a leftward curve ascending gently as it skirts the ridge ahead of you. Behind this ridge the sun will be dropping below the pines, while behind you the pale disc of the almost-full moon will already be high in the sky.

All around you are heather-trees, and rising between them, above and below you, Canary pines stand tall and straight; and carefully thinned to prevent the spread of fires. The occasional trees with evergreen leaves are wax-myrtles, ferns carpet the forest floor wherever sunlight falls, flowers and grasses line the path, butterflies flit, and the air is filled with birdsong.

After about a kilometre the peak of El Teide, the highest mountain in Spain, appears above the trees on your left, and, cloud permitting, the rest of Tenerife as well. If you look down to your left you can see the junction where your walk began.

Here the path rounds the end of the ridge and starts an overall curve to the right, and at around the point where the path to Igualero branches off to the left you will come back into the sunshine. Ignore this path, and the one to the right, and follow the sign to Alto de Garajonay 1.9 km.

Garajonay

In a short while the massive, flat-topped lava slab of La Forta-leza will appear on your left, with the village of Chipude below it. To the left of it you will see the island of El Hierro on the horizon, and over to its right the twin peaks of La Palma, usually floating on a sea of cloud. From this point onwards you will be able to watch the sunset - towards El Hierro in the winter, and towards La Palma in the summer.

If you continue along the forestry road, you pass a path leading down to La Laguna Grande and Chipude, and a little further on meet the road ascending from the main road to Alto de Garajonay. Turn right, and in 500 metres you will be standing on the summit of La Gomera, 1,487 m above sea level, and 144 m higher than Ben Nevis.

As daylight fades, moonlight takes over, silhouetting the trees and rocks and bringing a new kind of beauty to the forest and the landscape. And it is more than bright enough to light your home-ward stroll without stumbling.

An alternative way to return to your car is to walk down to the main road, turn right, and follow the tarmac for 1.2 km until the junction appears.

This sort of walk can, of course, be done just before a full moon in any westward facing place; and even without the sunset, a full-ish moon is bright enough to see your way along forestry roads and cart tracks.

And you can reassure your nervous companion that on La Gomera there are absolutely no

nasty beasties to jump out and frighten them whatsoever - just rabbits, mice, owls, and a great many bats.

A bat's existence depends on it being able to catch small flying insects while flying at high speed between the branches of trees in the pitch dark, so there's no need to duck.

the sea

THE CANARY CURRENT

The Canary Current is "a fast-moving, salt-water river flowing towards the setting sun, keeping eternal company with the trade-wind, westwards, westwards, air and water and all that floats and blows." So wrote Thor Heyerdahl, the Norwegian explorer famed for crossing oceans in flimsy craft.

It is also a cold current, and part of the great series of currents that create the North Atlantic Oscillation. It begins off the Straits of Gibraltar as an up-welling from the ocean depths, and flows south-west between the Canary Islands, warming up as it goes, before turning right and heading westwards for the Caribbean.

This current brought the first Canary Islanders on a one-way trip from Morocco more than two thousand years ago. Fifteen hundred years later it gave Columbus the impetus to discover America, and after that it gave the Canary Islands their importance as a staging post to the New World, until the age of steam made winds and currents irrelevant.

ROCK POOLS

A low-tide scramble around the rock pools can be very reward-ing, particularly in the morning and evening just after the full and new moons when the sea is at its lowest. As well as the familiar blennies and hermit-crabs, there are many baby bream and mullet, along with ornate wrasse with their turquoise bars. Sea hares, looking like giant crested slugs, slide along the rocks munching algae, and small octopuses hide in holes. It's best to choose a large pool with plenty of vege-tation, and to sit quietly beside it impersonating a rock - after a while the water will teem with life, while all around you rock-crabs will emerge.

BEACHES

The sand is 'black' because that's what La Gomera looks like once the sea has ground it up. But it's cleaner than most sand because, apart from the harbour beaches, the sea takes it away each winter and returns it thoroughly washed in the spring. Its disadvantage is that it becomes very hot - too hot to walk on - and you'll need sandals in the middle of the day. But don't leave them too close to the sea when you go for a swim.

The best sandy beaches are to be found in Valle Gran Rey, which has four and a sandy lagoon. San Sebastián has two, one a recent creation, and the beaches of Alojera and Playa de la Caleta near Hermigua usually have extensive sandy patches.

Otherwise the beaches consist of smoothed pebbles and stones, but in most cases their peace and unspoiled beauty make up for the lack of comfort.

RAMSHORN SHELLS
(Spirula spirula)

If you look among the flotsam along the tide-line you can often find ramshorn shells - small and delicate white spirals up to 2 cm across containing two or three loops - which are not shells at all.

Hold one up to the light and you'll see that it consists of separate chambers. It is in fact the skeleton of a Spirula, a small squid-like creature about 7 cm long that lives between 200 and 700 metres below the surface of the tropical oceans - the last surviving species of the great spiral-shelled 'cuttle fish' that swam in the Jurassic oceans around two hundred million years ago.

When they die and decompose, their skeletons float to the surface and drift with the winds and currents until they wash up on far distant beaches, where they puzzled people until 1912. Then the Danish biologist Johannes Schmidt, who was busy with his life's work of researching the life-cycle of the eel, hauled up some Spirula from the middle of the Atlantic, cut one open, and the mystery of the ramshorn shells was solved.

TIDE TABLE

Opposite is a rough guide to finding the times of high tides that I devised to help me with my fishing. It was compiled from my own observations, but is pretty much in accord with the accurate times published in local newspapers, and has proved to be close enough for most practical purposes.

Its most used and useful application is for establishing one's strategy for a day on the beach. If you know that the tide is ebbing, you can confidently stride to the front of the beach and lay your towel just above the mark of the last-highest wave; and if you know that the sea is coming up, you can settle yourself safely behind the last high tide mark and enjoy a bit of *schadenfreude* as the towels of the less well-informed are swept into the waves.

There are two high tides per day, and they occur about 12 hours and 25 minutes apart - or in other words, daytime high tides occur about 50 minutes later each day. And low tides occur about six hours after high tides.

At full and new moon the high tides are at roughly the same times, more or less between one-

thirty and two-thirty; and those at the quarter moons occur somewhere between seven-thirty and eight-thirty. And the highest high tides, and the lowest low tides, occur a couple of days after full and new moon.

All you need to find out is when the next/last full/new/quarter moon is/was - they are about seven days apart - and count forwards or backwards. Most of the wall-calendars in shops, bars, offices, etc., show the phases of the moon.

And remember that from the last Sunday in March until the last Sunday in October all the times are one hour later than GMT: which of course stands for Gomera Mean Time.

THE MOON   HIGH TIDES GMT

New & Full Moon	01.30-02.30
+1	02.00-03.00
+2	03.00-04.00
+3	03.30-04.30
+4	04.00-05.00
+5	05.00-06.00
+6	06.00-07.00
Quarter Moons	07.30-08.30
+1	08.30-09.30
+2	09.00-10.00
+3	10.00-11.00
+4	11.00-12.00
+5	12.00-01.00
+6	12.30-01.30

The Sea

EXCURSION BOATS & WHALE WATCHING

The main excursion boats, the **Tina** and **Siron**, operate out of Vueltas in Valle Gran Rey, and usually collect passengers from Playa Santiago as well. They offer an entertaining day at sea, and tickets can be purchased on the quay before departure. They usually leave at about ten, return at about five, provide a meal, snacks and drinks, and always pause in a cove where you can swim and fish.

When they leave the harbour they head north (right), and the thickness of the line of cloud above the horizon, known as *la barra*, indicates the roughness of the sea up there - although the duration of the northward leg is usually determined by the sea-worthiness of the passengers long before the state of the waves becomes an issue.

Los Órganos

Most times the boats manage to get as far as **Los Órganos**, a spectacular headland of hexagonal lava columns looking like organ pipes that is only visible from the sea; and if you can see below the surface, hammerhead sharks gather in this area to do their courting. If the sea is calm they continue around the island, but normally they head back south, past Valle Gran Rey to calmer seas, and drop anchor in a quiet bay while food is served.

The crews are constantly on the lookout for whales and dolphins, and will bring you among them whenever possible. The big birds you see skimming the waves offshore are shearwaters, and flying-fish and turtles sometimes put in an appearance.

For more intimate nautical jaunts, **Capitano Claudio** in Vueltas, Valle Gran Rey, offers whale-watching and fishing excursions in small boats, and also sailing trips on his yacht Triana.

The Sea

MARINE LIFE ON THE OPEN OCEAN

Fish that are fished can be found under 'Fishing'. This is a selection of aquatic life that may be seen above or close to the surface from the ferries and excursion boats.

Dolphins *(Delphinus delphis)*
The undisputed stars of the sea. They have an unaccountable liking for humans, and more often than not meet up with the excursion boats and put on an impromptu show. They seem to gain particular encouragement from whistles and the shrieks of delighted children as they leap and splash and race around the boat, until they suddenly decide show's-over and disappear into the depths. But they're not so popular with fishermen, because a hooked fish sends out distress signals that sound like a dinner-gong to a dolphin, and all the fisherman gets is the head.

Pilot Whales
(Globicephala melaena)
Often mistaken for dolphins, but they're not as playful, are larger and more solidly built, and don't have the dolphin's pointed nose.

Other Whales
The sea between the Canary Islands is very deep, up to four kilometres in places, and rich in fish and krill, making it a popular thoroughfare for these magnificent migratory monsters. But they're here to feed, and only surface when they have to, which is not very often. But if you're lucky, you will never forget it.

Flying Fish *(Exocoetus volitans)*
These are summer visitors, and can often be spotted zooming along below the surface like torpedoes before bursting into view. They fly to escape predators, with what is actually a

Pilot Whales

powered glide assisted by vigorous flapping of their out-sized pectoral fins. And if you can tear your eyes from the magic of their unexpected and iridescent appearance, you can often see a larger fish following their flight-path below the surface.

A great many other fish also leap out of the water to escape predators, including shoals of skipjack tuna, so keep your eyes peeled.

Hammerhead Shark
(Sphyrna zygaena)
This odd-looking shark is plentiful in the waters around Los Órganos, where the sea is deep enough for them to perform the spiralling dive that is part of their courtship ritual. If the water is calm, they can be seen swimming lazily below you; and they can grow to 4 metres and are notoriously bad-tempered.

Blue Shark *(Prionace glauca)*
These can also reach 4 metres, and like to cruise just below the surface with their dorsal fins sticking out of the water. They tend to follow the shoals of tuna and sometimes appear in great numbers - I once counted 41 while sailing from Valle Gran Rey to Playa Santiago.

Loggerhead Turtle
(Caretta caretta)
These are quite common between the islands, but are solitary and shy and will dive out of sight if you get too close.

Dolphins

The Sea

FISHING

The favoured bait in these parts is prawns *(gambas)*, along with squid *(calamar)* and mackerel *(caballa)*. Bread works for tiddlers, and also for mullet. The Canary Islands have no rivers, and therefore no muddy estuaries for worms to inhabit. The best tackle shop is Elyman in San Sebastián, but most ironmongers *(ferreterias)* sell the basics.

Harbours

These are the most popular fishing spots, 24 hours a day, and provide the widest variety of fish for the widest variety of anglers.

With a hand-line, a small hook, and bread for bait, children can amuse themselves for hours trying to catch the colourful damsel-fish and other small fish that browse the walls. Bogues *(bogas)* can be plentiful and are delicious if eaten as soon as you get them home, and at night an assortment of bream come in to feed. Almost every variety of fish has been pulled out of the harbours at some time or other, from barracudas to moray eels. Ledgering normally produces the biggest fish, including massive rays who do their courting in the harbours, but octopuses can anchor your line to the bottom, and there are many ropes and much rubbish, so it can be expensive on end-tackles.

Also, lurking in the sand, are the dreaded weevers *(arañas del mar)*. These can grow to 20 cm, are speckled blue and brown on the top and white underneath, have a receding jaw, and a small fin runs all the way along their back. They also have, at the back of their head, a black, retractable fan-like fin of poisonous spines, and poisonous spines on their gill-covers. If you catch one cut the line. If you get stung by one, even a small one, head straight for the nearest *Centro Medico*, as I can vouch that the pain rapidly becomes quite phenomenal. There they will give you the antidote, an injection of cortisone, and the pain will magically abate almost immediately.

Off the Rocks

This is the best daytime fishing, but also the most hazardous. As with the harbours, bogues and bream are the main source of entertainment, and derbios and guelly jacks as well. But weevers can infest sandy bottoms.

Off the Beaches

Fishing lore holds that the best fishing is to be had two hours before high-tide and one after, and this is particularly true from the beaches; although only at night once the swimmers have gone. But the night-time high-tides of summer can produce very large fish, including smooth-hound *(cazón)*, dogfish *(galludo)*, and other small sharks and rays, along with unidentified monsters that feel like you've snagged a submarine until your line breaks.

There are also various sorts of bream, which provide a satisfying breakfast, and at times large numbers of baby sharks, which should always be thrown back, as should all fish that you don't intend to eat.

Boat Fishing

Most of the local fishermen ledger with a hand-line for dentex, pandora, bream, combers, derbios, guelly jacks and triggerfish, or trail hooks for mackerel. They also hunt wahoos *(peto)*, a sort of large tuna, standing on the bow

Smooth-hounds

with a trident in one hand while controlling the tiller and throttle with a length of rope in the other, a very specialised skill.

The bigger boats catch skip-jack tuna by spraying water over the sea. This sounds like a shoal of small fish to the tuna, who flock to the boat in hope of a meal, where the only fish are on a hook attached to a strong line tied to the end of a bamboo rod.

Game Fishing
Marlin, swordfish and sharks are all out there for the Hemingways among you, and suitable boats can be usually found in the harbours of San Sebastián and Valle Gran Rey.

traditions

Fiestas

FIESTAS

Despite their overt Catholic pretensions, there seems to be a strong pre-Christian element lurking not far below the surface of many of the fiestas celebrated on La Gomera. Throughout their duration, which can be several days, vast numbers of exploding rockets reverberate around the barrancos, mingling with the mournful sounds of conch shells to create a din which is presumably intended to drive away evil spirits; while from sunset to dawn, amplified music blasts from the patio of the local church to ensure that nobody sleeps.

The objects of this strange form of veneration are statues representing Saints and an assortment of Virgins bedecked with fruits and flowers. These are carried shoulder-high around the streets, often preceded by dancers in traditional costumes, and serenaded with traditional songs accompanied by guitars, tambors and giant castanets called chácaras. And San Pedro and the Virgin del Carmen are taken for riotous trips on decorated fishing boats as well.

For folklorists, the music, dances and costumes that ac-

Virgin de Guadalupe

company the processing of the statues are a treasure trove of tangled cultures. The melodies and the phrasing of the songs have a distinctly North African feel, the percussion beats a restrained and steady 6/4, usually with a triplet on the second beat

of each bar, while the dancing, which consists mostly of dainty hops and turns with the arms raised above the head, has a restrained and almost courtly stateliness. But throughout this mélange runs an essential Gomeroness that is born of this island and owes nothing to anybody else's culture.

Culture aside, the fiestas are splendid occasions for having a good time. The secular part of the proceedings usually begins at around what the British call 'closing-time', there are normally at least two bands providing non-stop (mostly salsa) music until the sun reappears, and at least some of the many bars serve some kind of food.

The main winter fiesta, Los Reyes or Epiphany, lasts for three or four days around 6th January, which is when Christ-

Fiestas

mas was before the calendar was changed in 1582.

The main summer fiestas, each at least three days long, start on 13th June with San Antonio, followed by San Juan (the midsummer fire festval) on 24th, San Pedro on 29th, and after a brief pause the Fiesta de

San Pedro

Nuestra Señora del Carmen on 16th July, followed by Santiago (St James) on 25th; making six weeks during which very little work gets done.

And on 15th August, hundreds of people converge on Chipude, the highest village on the island, to celebrate the Virgin de Candelaria, the patron saint of the Canary Islands.

In addition, Agulo celebrates St Mark on 24th April, Alajeró processes Nuestra Señora de Buen Paso on 14th September, and almost every village has its own fiesta during the summer.

Moreover, every five years, 2003, 2008, etc., starting at the beginning of October, the Virgin of Guadalupe, La Gomera's patron saint, is taken from her lonely chapel above Punta Llana, north of San Sebastián, and carried or driven through every village on the island.

Virgin de Los Reyes

Fiestas

FIESTA DE LOS REYES
VALLE GRAN REY

141

El Silbo

EL SILBO

El Silbo (from *silbar* - to whistle) is the other language of La Gomera, and, as the name suggests, it consists entirely of whistling. The usual technique is to place the middle knuckle of the index or middle finger of one hand on the tip of the tongue, push it into one side of the mouth, and whistle through the other side - a technique that can take some time to learn. The intonation is controlled by the tongue, and can be modulated by the cup of the free hand.

It is a language in its own right, quite unique, unrelated to Spanish, and a bit of a mystery. There is no doubt that it evolved to enable communication across La Gomera's ravine-ridden terrain, much like yodelling in the Alps; and as it's not simply a whistled form of Spanish, it probably developed during the 1,500 years that the Guanches had the island to themselves. More than that nobody knows; although its continued existence supports the idea that the original natives of La Gomera were not entirely exterminated when the Spanish arrived.

El Silbo is now taught in the local schools, where it is a popular subject, particularly the homework. But even without the demonstrations put on for visitors, its sheer usefulness should prevent it from dying out. It can often be heard shrilling across the upper reaches of the barrancos as goatherds and toilers on terraces chat with each other and the villages below, messages can be passed across the island in minutes - and there are no batteries to recharge.

WILDLIFE

Like most islands, La Gomera has a large number of species that are exclusive to its shores. The majority are small insects, but there are a cricket, a mantis and a bee-eater like nobody else's, and all the lizards have evolved to be different from the rest.

ANIMALS

The Native Animals of La Gomera is the world's shortest book. There are none, and never have been. The only wild ones are rabbits, rats and mice, all introduced by man. Goats, however, wander free, and donkeys still carry things where four-wheel-drives can't reach.

Wildlife

Birds

La Gomera provides a great variety of habitats, from cliffs and coastal scrub to farmland and subtropical rainforest, and supports a wide variety of bird life. Far too many to describe, but here are some of the more notable species

PLAIN SWIFT
(Apus unicolor)
The swiftest of the swifts, they can easily attain 100kph, and are considered to be the best fliers that inhabit our planet. They are natives of the Canaries and Madeira, although they often winter in Africa, and from spring until autumn form wheeling, squealing flocks as they hunt insects with dare-devil aerobatics - often at head height. When they fly low, it is usually an indication that strong winds are imminent.

They nest in colonies, in holes in caves in the walls of the barrancos, well out of the reach of predators and the curious.

KESTREL
(Falco tinnunculus canariensis)

This is the Canary Islands' version of the hawk that hunts the sides of Europe's motorways; but only an ornithologist can tell the difference. Here, because of the vertical landscape, they can as often be seen from above as below; and thrive on the plentiful supply of lizards and mice.

BUZZARD
(Buteo buteo insularum)

The Spanish call it the mousetrap eagle, *aguila ratonera*, and it spends much of its time hovering over the edges of the forest looking for rodents. But when it's too cloudy up there it comes down to hunt in the barrancos, where it is constantly harassed by kestrels and swifts.

RAVEN *(Corvus corax)*

This all-black crow with a 64 cm wing-span is the biggest all-black bird in Europe, which with its deep croaking 'pruck-pruck' call makes it easy to identify.

In the springtime they give up their rather heavy style of flying and perform remarkable acrobatics, including flying upside-down, tumbling and nose-diving.

Springtime Ravens

Birds

CANARY
(Serinus canaria)

The bright-yellow canary that sings in cages has been carefully bred for more than five hundred years.

Their wild ancestors are less distinguished. The underside of the male is a bright yellow, but the female is much paler, and their upper parts are mostly grey/brown.

Although they sing no less beautifully and form choral flocks; and the best place to see and hear them is La Laguna Grande.

CANARY CHAFFINCH
(Fringilla coelebs tintillon)

Most often seen around the barbecue areas in the Parque Nacional, where they peck the crumbs from the tables, this local version of Europe's commonest finch differs by having a slate-blue mantle and a greenish rump.

CANARY GREY WAGTAIL
(Motacilla cinerea canariensis)

Wherever there is fresh water you will find the grey wagtail, which has the longest tail of all the wagtails.

But only their upper part is grey, their undersides are a bright yellow and they deserve a better name.

Birds

CANARY BLUETIT
(Parus caeruleus teneriffae)

La Gomera, Tenerife and Gran Canaria are home to this variety of bluetit, which differs from the European version in having a black instead of a blue cap and almost no white on its wings.

CANARY CHIFFCHAFF
(Phylloscopus collybita canariensis)

These insect-eating warblers, probably the most common bird on the island, are known as *mosquiteros*, and they do useful work picking bugs off the fruit trees. Around the coast they flit among the thickets of tamarisk, where it is dry and dusty, and if you want to see them more clearly, spray water over a nearby plant and they will come to bathe in the drops on the leaves.

WHITE-TAILED & BOLLE'S LAUREL PIGEONS
(Columba junoniae & C. bollii)

Two rare species of forest-dwelling pigeon that exist only on La Gomera, La Palma and Tenerife,

but are surviving well in the Parque Nacional. Bolle's lives among the trees, the white-tailed prefers cliffs and open spaces.

They are both mainly slate-grey with lighter tails and areas of metallic green around their heads, and Bolle's has pinkish-purple metallic bits as well.

BARBARY PARTRIDGE
(Alectoris barbara)

These small game-birds are usually seen flying noisily away from you after you've disturbed them while out walking. Hunting them is permitted on Sundays from the last Sunday in August until mid-November, which can make hiking nerve-racking.

Chiffchaffs

Birds

CORY'S SHEARWATER
(Calonestris diomedea)

Known locally as *pardelas*, they spend most of their lives at sea, either bobbing in large clusters, or gliding improbable distances with their wingtips clipping the waves. They are best seen from the ferries and excursion boats, and are larger and more graceful than gulls, with grey-brown wings and white undersides.

They only come to land during the breeding season, and then after dark, so you won't see them from the coast. But they nest in holes in the cliffs: and if, while enjoying a quiet nightcap on the terrace of your apartment, the sky above your head suddenly fills with banshee wails and swooping ghostly shapes, that's them courting.

OSPREY
(Pandion haliaetus)

The sea-eagle is a naturally rare bird that frequents the most out-of-the-way and inaccessible cliffs. The excursion boats will point out their nests. But they hunt for fish all around the coast, and can often be seen from the beaches, distinguishable from gulls by their powerful and determined wing-beats. They also hunt the stocked reservoirs, particularly the one by Las Rosas, and are partial to carp and goldfish.

Cory's Shearwater

LITTLE EGRET
(Egretta garzetta)

A small, pure-white heron with a black beak and legs, and yellow feet. It can often be seen elegantly plucking small fish from the rock pools at low tide.

Wildlife

Reptiles

THE GIANT LIZARD OF LA GOMERA
(Gallotia bravoana)

A few years ago a completely new and rather large species of lizard was discovered living quietly in the cliffs high above Valle Gran Rey, which caused quite a stir in the zoological world, because the last recorded sighting of it was in 1895 and it was assumed to have become extinct. It is known simply as El Lagarto Gigante de la Gomera, or the Giant Lizard of Gomera, and is currently being assessed by experts, and its population encouraged to increase, before being presented to the public.

A specially constructed, and discreetly located, study/breeding centre has been built below the cliffs where they are found, and the lizards who wander into the scientists' traps are brought here to be studied.

They only produce eggs once a year, and then only about five, which is enough to keep their

Female

Male

population stable in their restricted environment, but not enough to provide a tourist attraction. So they are being carefully bred, and there are now many healthy youngsters scurrying around in their incubators, safe from rats, feral cats and other predators.

Hopefully these will provide a population large enough to satisfy the needs of the scientists and visitors, and allow the rest of the lizards to continue to live undisturbed where only men on ropes can reach them, as they have done for the past few million years.

The largest specimens in captivity are 50 cm long and weigh 300 gm, and their keeper tells me they bite. But the skeleton of a 55-year-old has been found (they keep growing all their lives and their bones have annual growth rings like a tree) that would have weighed beween 5 and 6 kilos and been a formidable beast 130 cm long.

They have white throats, the male's becomes whiter and brighter during the breeding season, and he also has folds of skin like a collar around his neck.

Otherwise they are just large, brown, and extremely rare lizards, and more of a curiosity than an attraction, because they are shy creatures and spend most of their lives sitting quietly where you can't see them.

Reptiles

GOMERA LIZARD
(Gallotia galloti gomerae)

These are only to be found on La Gomera, a subspecies of the Tenerife lizard, and they are abundant and can be seen wherever there are rocks and stones. The males are dark grey/brown with blue spots on their throat and flanks, and can grow to 40 cm. The females, which look like a different species, are smaller and smoother with brown and ochre stripes. With a bit of patience you can feed them with scraps of bread, cheese, ham, dead flies, etc., and they are particularly fond of yoghurt.

GOLDEN SKINK
(Chalcides viridanus)

A shiny golden-brown lizard, endemic to La Gomera, Tenerife and El Hierro. It is smaller than the Gomera lizard - up to 9 cm - and can be found in the same sort of places, and also in dark, damp corners under rotting vegetation.

GOMERA GECKO
(Tarentola gomerensis)

This is La Gomera's own sub-species of gecko or house-lizard. Up to 9 cm long, they patrol the walls and ceilings at night eating insects, and it is considered lucky to have them in your home. In the daytime they hide behind fridges, water-heaters, pictures, etc., and have the disconcerting habit of communicating with what sounds like a quiet chuckle.

The secret of geckos' sticky feet has only recently been discovered, and it's not glue or suction-pads, it's *van der Waals' forces*. These are weak inter-molecular forces which occur when unbalanced electrical charges around molecules cause them to attract one another, and they are produced by literally billions of extremely tiny hair-like structures called setae on the pad of each gecko toe. Collectively they create enough adhesion to keep it from falling off the ceiling, even a glass one. And as well as having a practical grasp of molecular physics, they can also see in the dark and grow new tails.

And you can inform your nervous companion that a gecko is only dangerous if you sprout wings and buzz in front of its nose.

Reptiles

GREEN TREE FROG
(Hyla meridionalis)

About 5 cm long, they live in humid places such as gardens and banana plantations. For a tiny creature they have an extremely loud croak, and are more often heard than seen, usually between sunset and midnight.

COMMON FROG
(Rana perezii)

Twice the size of the tree frog, they live around reservoirs and water tanks, and croak day and night during the breeding season. But like all frogs they are good ventriloquists and difficult to find, as they can appear to be in several places at the same time.

GREEN TREE FROGS

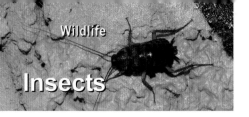

Insects

COCKROACH
(Periplaneta americana)

One must be honest - they're everywhere. Constant chemical warfare is waged against them, along with rolled-up newspapers and boots, but they're the world's greatest survivors and keep coming back. They can grow up to 4 cm, not counting their feelers, and are nocturnal; but apart from giving you an unpleasant surprise they're quite harmless, and on balance they're probably a good thing as they mostly eat rubbish.

The best way to keep them out of the house is to put food and rubbish away at night.

SLENDER MANTIS
(Hypsicorypha gracilis)

This twig-like insect flies like a disabled helicopter, but when it stands stock-still on a plant awaiting a passing fly with only its curiously pointed head moving it is elegant and imperious. It can grow to 8 cm, and when it has caught a fly it rotates it between its front legs and eats it like a corn-on-the-cob.

There are several other sorts of mantis on the island, including the famous Praying Mantis *(Mantis religiosa)*.

The small (3 cm), wingless Pale Mantis *(Pseudoyersinia pilipes)* lives in areas of dry shrubs, and its most distinguishing feature is that it exists only on La Gomera.

GRASSHOPPERS & CRICKETS *(Orthoptera)*

These are many and varied, particularly the grasshoppers in the high pastures. The Great Bush Cricket *(Calliphona alluaudi)* is a large forest dweller that often finds its way into gardens; the Mediterranean Bush Cricket is smaller and prefers cultivated land; and the loud one that you can never find and keeps you awake at night is usually the Field Cricket. The very big (6 cm) brown ones are African Locusts.

Great Bush Cricket

WINGLESS CRICKET
(Acrostira bellamyi)

If, while in a forest clearing, you encounter a large, yellow-brown, wingless grasshopper about 7 cm long, this will be Mrs Acrostira Bellamyi. Mr Acrostira Bellamyi is a mere 3 cm long, darker, and can often be seen riding around on his wife's back. The Acrostira Bellamyis dwell exclusively in the forests of La Gomera.

Wingless Cricket

RHINOCEROS BEETLE

(Oryctes nasicornis prolixus)

4 cm long and armour-plated, with a horn on the nose of the male, the rhinoceros beetle can be quite alarming when it noisily flies in of an evening. But it's quite harmless, and once it has landed it crawls around very slowly, allowing you to admire its remarkable structure.

They're a protected species throughout much of Europe, so once you've done looking, scoop it up gently and put it outside so it can continue looking for a mate. The adult beetles make a noise if you bother them.

They spend their first 3 years as larva, which grow 12 cm long as they munch their way through the trunks of dead palm trees.

Insects

DRAGONFLIES
(Odonata)

The big blue one 8 cm long is the Emperor Dragonfly. The smaller ones, around 5 cm long, are more properly called Darters and come in red, blue and yellow, while the African Darter is dark metallic blue with yellow markings. They're most prolific around the streams, but are often seen flitting about gardens, and are very useful eaters of pests.

GOMERA BEE-EATER
(Promachus gomerae)

A large (almost 3 cm) predatory fly that eats bees and any other insects that take its fancy.

They're most noticable when they're courting in the spring and summer. The female sits still on a rock or a twig, while the male, buzzing furiously, does a hovering dance around her with his long legs dangling.

Wildlife

Insects

BUTTERFLIES & MOTHS *(Lepidoptera)*

The largest (10 cm) and most beautiful butterfly in the Canary Islands is the orange and black Monarch *(Danaus plexippus)*, which emerges from a green chrysalis trimmed with gold, created by a black, yellow and white striped caterpillar. Their main source of food is the Curaço silkweed *(Asclepias curassavica)*.

They are natives of the west coast of America, where they migrate in huge flocks between Peru and Canada, and first appeared in the Canaries about a hundred years ago. But here they seem to have abandoned their instincts for flocking and travelling, and appear content just to float around looking pretty.

Monarch

Wildlife

Insects

Its slightly smaller relative, the African Monarch, can also be seen, along with Red Admirals, Painted Ladies, African Migrants, an assortment of white ones, and a great many smaller ones.

As you drive through the forests you can often see yellow and orange Cleopatras dancing in the roadside sunlight.

African Monarch

Red Admiral

Painted Lady

African Monarch caterpillars

The most common large moth in the Canaries is the Barbary Spurge Hawk Moth *(Hyles euphorbiae tithymali)*, an endemic whose brightly coloured caterpillars feed on the abundant spurges. It has a 7 cm wingspan and pink under-wings, and is often seen at dusk flitting from flower to flower. But in early February, when the peach trees are in blossom, it appears in the daytime; and then its hummingbird-like precision-hovering as it sips nectar through a tube as long as its body can be clearly appreciated.

The other large moths are the distinctive Death's Head Hawk Moth and the mottled brown Convolvulus Hawk Moth, both with 10 cm wingspans.

Amicta cabrerai

Barbary Spurge Hawk Moth

The Canary Islands are also home to a truly odd butterfly, known only by its Latin name, *Amicta cabrerai*. The male is a small and inconspicuous dark-brown butterfly about 15 mm long, but the female remains a caterpillar all her life; and instead of growing wings, she encases herself in a neat and relatively massive cocoon of tiny twigs that she cements together, and this she hauls around as she eats and lays her eggs.

plantlife

Plantlife

PLANTLIFE

Before I go any further, if you are seriously interested in botany, I unhesitatingly recommend *Natural History of the Canary Islands: La Gomera* by David Bramwell and Juan Manuel López. This is the definitive guide, and includes all the plants that exist only on La Gomera. The number of 'endemics' - species that are found here and nowhere else - is quite remarkable. There are at least 44, including 8 varieties of houseleek, and the island is host to at least another 50 plants that are exclusive to the Western Canary Islands.

The following are a selection of those plants that visitors most often ask about.

HOUSELEEK
(Aeonium various)

There are 60 species of houseleek in the Canaries, most of which produce rosettes of succulent leaves, sometimes on the end of a stalk, but most distinctively on rockfaces, and sometimes on the trunks of palm trees.

AGAVE
(Agave americana)

Originally from Mexico, and commonly known as the 'century plant' (and locally as *la pitera*), it grows wild over much of the island. After about ten to fifteen years it produces clusters of yellow flowers on a tall stalk that can be 12 m high, after which it dies. Its thick fleshy leaves, which have lethally sharp points, are used as fodder and produce a useful fibre; the wide base of the flower stalk can be used for the body of an African-type drum; and the long straight bit can be hollowed out and made into an 'authentic' Gomero digeridoo.

ALOE VERA
(Aloe vera)

Alexander the Great once conquered an island because it was covered with these plants, which he used for healing the wounds of his troops. Nowadays, industries and mountains of literature are devoted to promoting its medicinal powers, which are indeed remarkable, and well tried and tested; the problem being that it loses much of its healing power 24 hours after being cut no matter how you process it. But this is not a problem on La Gomera, where it grows wild and most gardens have a plant or two.

The gel in its spears disinfects and rapidly heals wounds, soothes insect bites, and is particularly effective in treating burns, especially sunburn - instructions for which follow:

1. Cut off a spear close to the base.
2. Trim the sides and tip.
3. Cut it into sections and divide them to reveal the gel.
4. Rub the gel over the affected area and leave to dry.
5. Wash your hands thoroughly as the gel is extremely bitter - although some people manage to use it as a mouthwash and eat it.

Plantlife

PRICKLY PEAR CACTUS/COCHINEAL
(Opunta ficus-indica/Dactylopius coccus)

Also known as the India Fig or Tunera, its fruit (*higos picos*) are a local delicacy; but on no account attempt to pick then with your bare hands as they are dotted with tiny rosettes of very sharp hair-thin thorns. The locals use a glove or a piece of thick cloth, then immerse them in a bucket of water and remove the thorns by rubbing them with a stick. They then cut off the top and bottom, split the side, peel back the thick skin, and eat the ball of flesh and pips in the middle.

They were brought to the Canary Islands from Mexico-way in the 1820s, along with the formerly-important cochineal insect.

This is a dark-grey, soft, sap-sucking mealy-bug that lives in colonies on the surface of the plant, and produces what looks like white mould to protect itself from predators and the sun. If you squash one, you will observe that its insides are crimson, and until chemists invented alternatives in the 1870s this was the main source of red dye, known as carmine. Nowadays, disconcertingly, its main use is as a food colouring and in cosmetics.

CASTOR-OIL PLANT
(Ricinus communis)

Known locally as *tartago*, this plant grows wild and has been used by man for thousands of years. The oil extracted from its seeds is famed as a laxative, and is also used as a lubricant and in making soap. These seeds are rather attractive, looking like small beetles, and no two are alike; and when they are ripe the seed-pods burst with a sharp 'crack', firing them a considerable distance.

However, the rest of the plant is extremely poisonous. An insecticide is made from the leaves, and it is the source of the deadly poison 'ricin' much loved by terrorists: so think twice about taking the pretty seeds home with you.

CANARY DATE PALM
(Phoenix canariensis)

This ubiquitous native of the Canaries is immensely useful, and La Gomera has more of them than any other island.

Its fruit and foliage, cut off with a very sharp knife lashed to a very long length of cane, are used for animal-feed. Its fronds can be woven into baskets, mats and hats, or laid thick and weighted with stones to make waterproof roofing - now used mostly for goatsheds. And the spray of fine twigs that bears the fruit, tied together with a piece of wire, makes a very effective broom.

But only on La Gomera did they discover that it also produces a delicious sap, and work out how to tap it - by shinning up the trunk, hacking out the middle of the crown, and siphoning it off as it wells up into the hole; a process that the tree normally and surprisingly recovers from. This sap is called *guarapo*, has an exquisite aromatic taste quite unlike anything else, and blends perfectly with rum or whisky; but unfortunately it doesn't keep. It can however be frozen, and if you are lucky enough to be given some it will probably be as a solid lump in a fizzy-drink bottle, and should be drunk as it melts. But normally it is boiled down to a thick syrup called *miel de palma*, or palm honey, which keeps longer and is also delicious, and can be purchased in the local shops.

CANE
(Arundo donax)

Until recently cane, *caña*, played a useful part in the economy of La Gomera. Growing where nothing else would grow, particularly along the usually bone-dry and rocky stream beds, its leaves fed goats and donkeys, and its stalks were cut and tied in big bundles and exported to hold up the raspberries and dahlias of northern Europe. It is still used for fodder, and for propping up local plants, but its export markets switched to plastic plant-props and it is rapidly becoming a pest.

Its dense thickets of tall stalks crowned with feathery flowers add to the exotic beauty of the island, and it is worth finding your way into a clump when it is windy just to listen to the rattling, creaking din. But they can fuel terrifyingly intense and fast-moving fires, and their powerful tubers destroy terrace walls and have a particular skill in invading and blocking sewerage pipes.

Plantlife

BANANAS
(Musa acuminata)

The most remarkable fact about the banana is that it hasn't had sex for about ten thousand years.

The wild banana, a giant plant living in the jungles of south-east Asia, bears a virtually inedible fruit that is mostly a mass of hard seeds. But sometimes it produces sterile and seedless offspring, and these the Stone Age plant breeders propagated by replanting the small plantlets that sprout from their bases, a process that has continued without a break to produce the wide variety of bananas eaten today.

The variety grown in the Canaries, the Dwarf Cavendish, is small, sweet and wind-resistant, and was discovered in Southern China in the 19th century. The plant has a productive lifetime of about 30 years, producing a succession of plantlets that each bear a single bunch of bananas. There are normally three plantlets visible; a chopped-off trunk known as the grandmother, the mother bearing the fruit, and the daughter, or daughters, sprouting from the base. A little before the fruit turn yellow they are covered with a special plastic bag that prevents them from ripening further, because they are harvested when they are green and hard to give them a better chance of arriving at the greengrocer's undamaged.

PAPAYA
(Carica papaya)

Otherwise known as the Paw-paw, this ungainly tree sheds its leaves as it grows, leaving the fruit to grow on the bare trunk where they hang like a cluster of misshapen balloons. The fruit, as well as being delicious with a squeeze of lemon, are an extremely good aid to digestion, as they contain the enzyme papain, which is used in stomach medicines and to tenderise meat.

ORANGES & LEMONS
(Citrus sinensis & Citrus limon)

Originally from China, these trees have been cultivated for thousands of years. On most varieties the fruit ripen in December and January, and in February and March their white blossom fills the barrancos with a heady fragrance.

LOQUAT
(Eriobotrya japonica)

A native of Japan, this drought-resistant tree, known locally as *níspero*, produces bunches of yellow olive-sized fruit for the first three months of the year. These are sweet but slightly acidic, although the less water a tree gets the sweeter the fruit, and are best eaten straight from the tree as they bruise easily; which is why you seldom see them in shops. Each fruit usually contains three nut-like seeds which germinate readily, with the result that most trees are semi-wild, and it is probably the only fruit you can pluck as you pass by without somebody shouting at you.

Plantlife

AVOCADO
(Persea americana)

There are many varieties of this easy to grow evergreen tree, some tall and stately, others thin and scraggly, and likewise many shapes and sizes of fruit, from round purple ones the size of tennis balls to giant green pears that provide a meal for two. Most fruit ripen in the last three months of the year, and the rich taste of a freshly picked ripe avocado, *aguacate*, bears little comparison to those which ripen on super-market shelves.

MANGO
(Mangifera indica)

The most widespread variety of mango on La Gomera is small, deliciously sweet and juicy, and full of fibres that catch between your teeth. Most of them start to ripen at the end of August creating a glut, and I have yet to find a way of eating them without getting into an enjoyably sticky mess. They grow on medium-sized trees which, like avocados, produce shiny purple/brown leaves that slowly become green.

The more conventional mangoes, larger and fibre-free but not as sweet, are more carefully cultivated, on bush-like trees behind secure fences, and produce fruit all the year round.

CASSIA
(Cassia didymobotrya)

Known as the peanut butter cassia because of the smell of its long spikes of yellow flowers, and a popular garden plant because of their beauty, this is an easy to grow shrub from tropical Africa.

It is also the source of food for the caterpillars of the African Migrant butterfly *(Catopsilia florella)*, which are bright yellow if they eat the flowers, and bright green if they eat the leaves.

African Migrants

Plantlife

MUSHROOMS AND TOADSTOOLS *(Fungi)*

There is usually an abundance of mushrooms and toadstools following the first heavy rain of the winter, particularly in the forest and among the bushes of the surrounding scrubland.

Field-mushrooms, boletes, chanterelles, blewits, brittle-gills, puffballs, etc., are all there for the finding; truffles too if you know where to look or have a pig with you, and morels in the spring. If you're an experienced mushroom gatherer, and it rains while you´re here, I don't need to tell you what to do. If you don't know what's what, stick to taking photos or buy a good book - for as somebody once said: "All mushrooms are edible, but some only once!"

Those illustrated are pretty and poisonous. The fly agaric is so called because if you chop it up small and put it in a saucer of milk it attracts flies, which then keel over completely stoned, buzz feebly while waving their legs in the air, and can be swept up.

Fly Agaric *(Amanita muscaria)*

Plantlife

Gomera Sea-Lavender

WILD FLOWERS

From around February until about June, a spectacular profusion of wild flowers covers the open ground, particularly the high pastures around the Parque Nacional and along the sides of the roads, and especially after a wet winter.

Swathes of magenta sweet-peas lie among pastures of assorted yellow and white flowers threaded with pink convolvulus, poppies create blazes of red on the high sides of the barrancos, mounds of Paris daisies rise among the rocks, sow-thistles produce great sprays of dandelion-like flowers around the forest margins, to name but a few.

But if you want to do more than simply enjoy this colourful ebullience of nature, I have once again to refer you to the works of David Bramwell, this time his *Flora of the Canary Islands*.

Asphodel

Gomera Bugloss

Gomera Spurge

Ortuño's Sow-Thistle

Sweetpeas

practical

PLEASE READ THESE PAGES

La Gomera is a crumbling lump of rock far out in the Atlantic Ocean, and its wild and rugged beauty is replete with danger. If you stick to the beaten track, treat the ocean with the respect it deserves, and generally exercise common sense, you will come to no harm - if you try to push your luck, La Gomera can be quite merciless.

THE SEA

Don't be deceived by other swimmers!
From November until Easter the only people in the sea are foreigners. The locals not only consider it too cold, but far too dangerous, and with very good reason, as the waves and currents can be, and too often are, lethal. But don't expect to see any warning signs. The stated policy of the Canary Islands' local governments is that they, and I quote, "will not erect warning signs, as they tarnish the image of the area and discourage tourists from visiting."

That said, the harbour beaches in San Sebastián and Valle Gran Rey, and Valle Gran Rey's Charco del Conde (The Baby Beach), are almost always calm and sandy and safe for children, and for most of the year even the more exposed beaches can be, and are, safely enjoyed.

It's always a good idea before going for a swim to settle yourself on the beach and check out what the sea's up to, and how the other swimmers are faring - the biggest waves come at about twenty-minute intervals, sometimes from an otherwise calm sea. And if you're not sure about it, you're probably right.

THE LAND

It may not look like it, but the footpaths really do follow the most direct and safest routes, and most accidents happen to people who try to find short-cuts. And don't try rock-climbing, or terrace-wall climbing, the cause of most other accidents. Also, remember that it is easier to lose your footing when going downhill.

It is important to bear in mind that darkness occurs about twenty minutes after sunset. This is considerably quicker than in Northern Europe, and catches many visitors by surprise. Therefore, do not select a romantic

spot from which to watch the sunset that is more than twenty minutes walk from your car or street lighting; unless, of course, you take a torch or there is a moon. If you do find yourself caught out, spend the last of the daylight finding the least uncomfortable sheltered spot in which to spend the night - walking in the dark is extremely hazardous.

THE WIND

Strong winds can dislodge stones from cliffs and dead fronds from palm trees - so when it's very windy it's best to stay in the open, or indoors.

THE SUN

This is the usual boring warning. I know - you've come here to get a tan, and at every turn there are people wittering on about how dangerous the sun is - and yet you're surrounded by enviably bronzed people, so surely it can't be all *that* dangerous.

The fact is, you don't see the people who've cooked themselves, except on the day they're overdoing it, because for the rest of their holidays they're indoors and in pain. But you can spot them at the airport on the way home - miserable-looking red and white faces, sometimes with bits of skin hanging off them.

Softlee softlee getee brownee - there's no other way!

COLD & WET

A little over half the water needed for the forests of the lush Parque Nacional falls as rain. The rest condenses on the leaves and needles from the clouds which cover it for much of the time, and the wind and the altitude accent the chill factor. Apart from the summer months, once you pass the tree-line it is advisable to have a waterproof, pullover and grown-up trousers handy.

FIRE

If you see smoke wafting out from under the tiles of small buildings in the villages, don't call the fire-brigade, this is how they smoke cheese in these parts.

If, however, you see an un-controlled fire anywhere in the countryside, particularly in the summer months, no matter how small, and you can't put it out, raise the alarm as quickly as possible. The word for fire is *fuego*, shout it and point. Your reward could be to witness heli-copters emptying giant red buck-ets of water over it, which they refill from the nearest reservoir or the sea, and small aircraft dive-bombing it with CO_2 gas.

Getting About

FERRIES

The mainstay of La Gomera's connections to the outside world is the Ferry Gomera, a car-ferry currently labelled 'Fred Olsen Express' which plies between San Sebastián de la Gomera and Los Cristianos on Tenerife. The Fred Olsen Line has provided this service for more than seventy years, the ferries have all been called Benchijigua - the unpronounceable name of a village owned by the Olsen family - and the road to the harbour in San Sebastián is called Paseo Fred Olsen.

The latest Ferry Gomera is a giant catamaran, enclosed and air-conditioned, that speeds you between the islands in 45 minutes. It currently makes six return journeys a day. The first and last departures from San Sebastián are at about 7am and 7pm respectively, and from Los Cristianos at about 8am and 8pm.

Trasmediterránea - or Trasmed - the Spanish national ferry company, offers two trips each way per day on La Isla de la Gomera, a car-ferry that sails between Los Cristianos and the outermost island of El Hierro, and calls in at San Sebastián en route. This takes 75 minutes, but it's a more conventional boat, and you can walk the decks and lean on the rail and look for dolphins.

Both these ferries have luggage-carts parked on the quay before departure, clearly marked, in which you can put your baggage to save lugging it up the gangway. It is important to retrieve it quickly from the Trasmed luggage-cart, or it will continue to El Hierro.

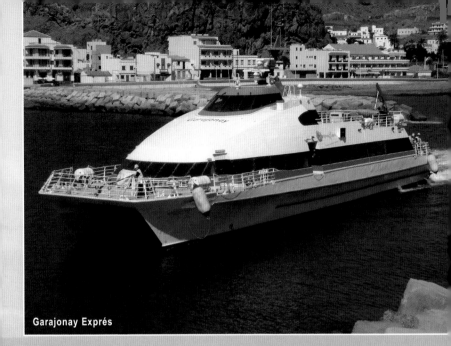

Garajonay Exprés

The newest of the ferries, the Garajonay Exprés, is a high-speed, people-only catamaran service based in Valle Gran Rey. It plies between Vueltas in Valle Gran Rey and Los Cristianos three times a day, calling in at San Sebastián and Playa Santiago en route. It is essentially an aquatic bus-service, and is the cheapest and most direct way to travel. The first and last depart-ures from Valle Gran Rey are about 7am and 5pm respect-ively, and from Los Cristianos about 9am and 7pm. This service, however, is the first to be affected when the sea gets rough.

The exact times of the ferries can be found at the harbours, infor-mation centres, and on the usual leaflets and notice-boards.

La Gomera

Tenerife

Valle Gran Rey

Los Cristianos

San Sebastián

Playa Santiago

Getting About

BUSES

BUSES

If you ask a taxi-driver where you can catch a bus, he will probably tell you that there are no buses on La Gomera and invite you to step into his cab. Here a bus is called a *guagua* - pronounced gwa-gwa. This was originally a Quechua word (the language of the Incas) for a 'baby', but in the Canary Islands and Cuba it has somehow come to mean a 'municipal bus' - which is something that Spaniards from the Peninsula find highly amusing.

The guaguas run from San Sebastián to all the main towns, and their times tie in with the Ferry Gomera. As it pulls into the harbour they wait side-by-side on the quay; blue, air-conditioned, Servicio Regular Gomera SL on their sides, and cards in their front windows indicating their destinations. And they depart from their destinations in time to catch the next ferry.

Their exact times can be found in the same sort of places as the ferry times, and also on the walls of bars and shops.

TAXIS

These are white with a green light and 123 on their roofs, and generally drive too fast; but an in-car conversation in English incorporating the word vomit - the Spanish word is *vomitar* - usually slows them down without confrontation. They are invaluable for getting back to base after a long cross-country walk, but don't leave it too late as most of them knock off at nine-o'clock in the evening.

CARS

Cars for hire are increasingly plentiful on La Gomera, particularly around the harbour of San Sebastián, and in Valle Gran Rey and Playa Santiago.

There are six filling-stations on the island - San Sebastián, Playa Santiago, Valle Gran Rey, Vallehermoso, Hermigua, and

close by Chipude in the village of Apartaderos. They open at 8am and close at 9pm, except on Sundays when they close at 2pm.

TWO WHEELS

Motorbikes, scooters and bicycles can be hired in Valle Gran Rey.

There is a phenomenon in these parts known as the English accident. These occur when, while driving along a winding country lane, you suddenly find a hire-car heading towards you on your side of the road and realise that the driver is fully expecting you to get out of his way.

If you're British, it's very easy, when the road is deserted and you're pootling along enjoying the views, to instinctively pull over to the left when a car comes the other way.

Don't become a statistic!

Food

SELF-CATERING

As most of the accommodation on La Gomera is self-catering, most of this section is a guide to the wrinkles of keeping yourself watered and fed.

The tap water varies from place to place, but it is all technically drinkable. Usually the higher you are the better the taste, with pure spring-water in the upper villages and chemical soup by the sea. The Spanish word for hot is *caliente*, cold is *frío* - so the hot-water tap has a C on it, and the cold an F.

The gas used for cooking and heating water is butane and comes in large metal bottles. If it runs out contact your landlord/ lady. Or you can exchange the empty bottle for a full one at the nearest petrol station - they weigh about 30 kg.

The coffee-pot can be a bit of a mystery. Fill the lower section with water to the safety-valve: put in the tray, which should remain dry, and fill it with ground coffee *(café molido)*: screw on the top and place the pot on the smallest gas ring. When it makes a sputtering sound your coffee is ready.

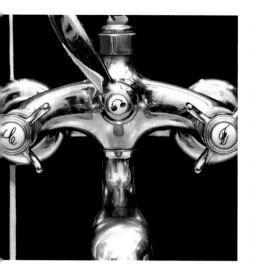

FOOD SHOPPING

Most shops open 9-10ish, close 1-2ish, open again 4-5ish, and close again 8-9ish.

As a general rule, if fruit and veg look slightly less than perfect, are of assorted shapes and sizes, and in boxes that have been used before, then they are locally grown and full of flavour, vitamins, minerals and all that good stuff.

Locally grown fruit include oranges, lemons, bananas, avocados, guavas, mangoes, papayas, passion-fruit and figs; and the vegetables include

potatoes, carrots, sweet-potatoes, onions, peppers, etc. Most food shops sell locally laid eggs, and also fresh goat's milk cheese *(queso de cabra)*. Bread, in the form of rolls and small brown loaves, is locally baked.

Local products include *almogrote* - a 'spread' made with mature goat-cheese and red peppers; *miel de palma* - a syrup made from palm-tree sap; and *gofio* - a toasted cornflour.

Fresh fish can be bought from refrigerated vans with loudspeakers on their roofs that drive around the valleys playing music and advertising the days catch. They usually have tuna *(albacore)*, mackerel *(caballa)* and sardines, as well as white-fish and sometimes moray eels.

Decent tea is almost impossible to find, and what there is is pricey - best bring your own next time.

Almost all milk is UHT. The most milk-like milk to the English palate is Leche Asturiana, from the lush pastures in the north of Spain, and the bits sometimes floating in their Leche Entera (whole-milk - in the red cartons) are cream.

EATING OUT

I can make no claim to having eaten in all the restaurants, nor drunk in all the bars, of La Gomera, so apart from the odd mention in the Tour Around the Island I make no attempt at a Gomera Good Food Guide.

Suffice to say that there are plenty of places to eat, particularly in Valle Gran Rey and San Sebastián; that the quality of the food is generally above average and less 'processed' than in Europe; and that the prices will come as a pleasant surprise.

Most of the bar-restaurantes in the rural areas (which sometimes double as the village shop) are family-run with the accent on home-cooking, but the kitchens tend to close soon after sunset.

A typical menu will include *potaje de berros* (water-cress soup); *carne frito* (fried meat) and *chuletas* (chops) - usually *cerdo* (pork) and often local and fresh; *carne de cabra* (goat meat); *conejo* (rabbit); *chocos* (cuttlefish); *pescado* (fish); and *leche asada* (a local version of crème caramel). The *papas* (potatoes) are either *fritas* (chips) or *arrugadas* (boiled and salted).

After ordering a meal, a basket containing your cutlery and bread will be placed on the table, along with small pots of sauce called *mojo* to eat with the bread while you're waiting. Red mojo is made with hot peppers and should be eaten carefully; green mojo is made with fresh coriander and is mild; *alioli* is a garlic mayonnaise.

In the towns you have everything from up-market Gomero to Malay and Arabian, and the standard of pizzas is very high. Many restaurants will do takeaway *(para llevar)* if you ask.

Mojo

CAFÉS

Most of the cafés serve tapas - small plates of prepared food that you can select from trays in display cabinets on the bar. They also have well-filled bread rolls called *bocadillos*, sandwiches, and often a superb and filling potato salad called *ensaladilla*.

A black coffee is a *café solo*, a white coffee is a *café con leche*, and you can normally get fresh orange juice - *zumo de naranja* (pronounced naranka). They often have a selection of fresh *zumos* (fruit juices) and *batidos* (milk-shakes). *Helado* is ice-cream. If you want tea *(té)* it's best drunk with lemon *(con limón)* as you've no chance of a decent 'cuppa'.

MEDICAL

In an emergency dial **112** (1+1=2 is the mnemonic), there should be an English-speaking operator available. **Remember to say that you are on La Gomera**, as the Emergency Control Centre is on Tenerife.

If you are reading this in the UK before coming to La Gomera, pop down to the Post Office and get an E111, and keep it and a photocopy with your passport. This is the form that entitles you to the same free health-service benefits that you enjoy in the UK. It costs nothing, lasts indefinitely, and can save you a fortune - not least in not having to pay for unnecessary private insurance.

The Spanish health-service is on a par with the NHS, and has the same failings and problems; but generally the treatment is excellent and friendly, and you need have no fears.

Health-service doctors and emergency treatment can be found in the health centres - **Centro de Salud** - in Valle Gran Rey, Santiago, Vallehermoso, Agulo and Hermigua, and in the hospital in San Sebastián. If necessary, a helicopter can whisk you to the large teaching-hospital in Santa Cruz de Tenerife, which has the full array of up-to-date resources.

Unlike the NHS, the Spanish expect that whenever possible a relative or close friend stays with the patient, often sleeping on the floor by the bed. Quite apart from reducing the work-load of the nurses, it eases the stress of being in hospital and speeds recovery.

For minor complaints it is best to have a chat with a chemist at a *farmacia*. They have greater discretionary powers than British chemists, and are allowed to sell you a wide range of medicines without a prescription, including antibiotics and powerful pain-killers, provided they are satisfied it is the correct treatment.

For sunburn: see Aloe Vera.

BANKING

If you require more than a cash-point, and particularly if you want to transfer cash or do any kind of business on La Gomera, look for a BBVA, La Caixa or Banco Santander. These are modern, international banks which provide facilities to a normal European standard, and close at 2pm. The Cajas, Caja Canarias and Caja Rural, have modern façades, but are old-style provincial banks with old-style habits and can be very frustrating.

POST

Letter-boxes are bright yellow with a cream, silver or blue crown and trumpet motif. Stamps can be bought when you purchase postcards, or from the Correos (post office).

SIESTA

Breaking the day into two chunks and having a snooze in the middle is fundamental to the Gomero way of life, and an extremely civilised habit that is quite easy to adapt to. Siesta normally lasts three hours, 1pm-4pm or 2pm-5pm.

USEFUL TELEPHONE NUMBERS

Ambulance, Fire & General Emergencies	**112**
Police/Guardia Civil	062
Hospital - San Sebastián	922 14 02 00
British Consulate	922 28 68 63
Calls to UK	00 44

TAXIS

San Sebastián	922 87 05 24
Playa Santiago	922 89 50 22
Valle Gran Rey	922 80 50 58
Vallehermoso	922 80 02 79
Hermigua	922 88 00 47
Agulo	922 80 10 74

TOURIST INFORMATION OFFICES

San Sebastián	922 14 15 12
Playa Santiago	922 89 56 50
Valle Gran Rey	922 80 54 58

FERRIES

Fred Olsen	922 87 10 07
Trasmediterránea	922 87 13 24
Garajonay Exprés	922 80 70 77

FLIGHTS TO UK

The Travel Shop, Los Cristianos	922 79 37 18/22

USEFUL WORDS

If you have a smattering of Spanish, you will notice that the language spoken on La Gomera bears the same sort of relationship to Castilian Spanish that Glaswegian does to the Queen's English. The 's's tend to be inaudible, so *gracias* becomes *gracia* and *adiós* becomes *adió*, etc: but more confusingly *pescado* (fish) sounds like *pecado* (sin). Also the 'th' sound is never used, so when you want a beer you can pronounce *cerveza* in the English manner instead of struggling with 'thervetha'.

Adiós	Goodbye, but also used as a passing hello - it means 'To God'.
Agua	Water
Aguacate	Avocado
Alemán	German
Anchoas	Anchovies
Apartamento	Apartment
Asado	Roasted
Atún	Tuna
Ayuntamiento	Town hall
Barco	Boat
Barranco	Valley/ravine/gulley
Bar-Restaurante	A bar that serves food when the kitchen's open
Batido	Milkshake
Berros	Watercress
Bocadillo	Filled bread roll
Boquerones	Pickled anchovies
Broma	Joke
Buen provecho	Good appetite
Burro	Donkey
Buzón	Letter-box
Caballa	Mackerel
Caballero	Gentleman

Caballeros	Gents
Caballo	Horse
Cabra	Goat
Café	Coffee & café
Caliente	Hot
Camino	Footpath
Caña	Cane/A small glass of draught beer
Carne	Meat
Carne de Res	Beef
Carretera	Road
Casa	House
Centro de Salud	Medical Centre
Cerdo	Pork
Cerveza	Beer
Chocos	Cuttle-fish
Chorizo	Salami
Chuletas	Chops
Coche	Car
Conejo	Rabbit
Copa	Cup/Wine glass
Cordero	Lamb
Correos	Post-office
Cuenta	Bill
Derecha	Right
Ermita	Chapel
Estrella	Star
Farmacia	Chemist
Ferretería	Ironmongers
Fresco	Fresh
Frio	Cold
Frito	Fried
Gasoil	Diesel

USEFUL WORDS

Gasolina	Petrol
Gato	Cat
Gofio	Toasted cornflour
Gracias	Thank you
Guagua	Bus
Guarapo	Palm-tree sap
Helado	Ice-cream
Hielo	Ice
Huevos	Eggs
Inglés	English
Izquierda	Left
Jabón	Soap
Jamón	Ham
Jarra	Jug/A large glass of draught beer
Lagarto	Lizard
Leche	Milk
Librería	Bookshop
Limón	Lemon
Llave	Key
Lomo	Back-bacon/Ridge
Luna	Moon
Mar	Sea
Melocotón	Peach
Mesa	Table
Miel de Palma	Palm Honey - concentrated palm-tree sap
Mira	Look!
Mirador	A place from which to enjoy a spectacular view
Moto	Motorbike
Naranja	Orange
Obras	Works, as in Road-works

Palmera	Palm tree
Pan	Bread
Papas arrugadas	Salted boiled potatoes
Papas fritas	Chips & crisps
Parranda	An evening of traditional music
Periódico	Newspaper
Perro	Dog
Perro caliente	Hotdog
Pescado	Fish - on a plate
Pez	Fish - in the water
Plancha	Hotplate/griddle
Platano	Banana
Playa	Beach
Plomo	Lead
Pollo	Chicken
Potaje	Thick vegetable soup
Pulpo	Octopus
Queso	Cheese
Refresco	Soft drink
Salchicha	Sausage
Servicios	Toilets
Sol	Sun
Solomillo	Fillet steak
Sopa	Soup
Tapas	Snacks
Té	Tea
Vaso	Glass
Vino del país	Local wine
Vino tinto/rosado/blanco	Red/rosé/white wine,
Zapato	Shoe
Zumería	Juice-bar
Zumo	Juice

Natural History of the Canary Islands: La Gomera - David Bramwell and Juan Manuel López. Editorial Rueda. (English) *A thorough guide to the plants and wildlife of the island, with the accent on the endemics.*

Flora of the Canary Islands - David Bramwell. Editorial Rueda. (English) *Like the above, but covering all the islands and without the fauna.*

The Edge of the Sea - Rachel Carson. Penguin. (English) *Fifty years old and still the definitive guide to the seashore - a well-informed, chatty, and very readable account of the world between the tides - the perfect beach book in every sense.*

Peces de Canarias: Guía Submarina - J González, C Hernández, P Marrero & E Rapp. Francisco Lemur Editor. (Spanish) *Underwater pics of the fish around the islands, with a list of their English names at the back.*

Guía de las Aves de las Islas Canarias - José Manuel Moreno. Editorial Interinsular Canaria. (Spanish) *A complete guide to the birds of the Canaries, both those which nest here and those which pass through; including their English names, in the index as well.*

Los Volcanes de las Islas Canarias/Canarian Volcanoes - Tenerife - Vicente Araña & Juan C Carracedo. Editorial Rueda. (Spanish/English) *A good explanation of the forces that created these islands, but the quality of the translation leaves a lot to be desired.*

La Gomera: 46 Bergwanderungen in ursprünglicher Natur - Rüdiger Steuer. Goldstadtverlag. (German) *A comprehensive walking guide - in German. But the maps are mostly excellent, and with help from the photos a serious hiker should be able to figure the rest out.*

Alternative Gomera - Nicholas Albury. Institute for Social Inventions. (English) *A dedicated walking guide; and an entertainingly personal conducted tour along a great many of the footpaths and through most of the towns and villages of the island. It is packed with practical advice and useful information, and has rudimentary maps but no photos. And although limited by being informed mostly from January visits, it is a very useful companion to the Rüdiger Steuer book, and a decidedly British effort.*

Walk! La Gomera - David & Ros Brawn. Discovery Walking Guides. (English) *Written by a pair of enthusiastic hikers, full of puff and sweat and healthy exercise, but virtually unreadable and difficult to follow - more 'What we did on our holidays' than practical advice. And the maps are inaccurate, and the photos are poor.*

INDEX

INDEX

INDEX